Academic Skills
Reading, Writing, and Study Skills

LEVEL 3   **Student's Book**

Sarah Philpot and Lesley Curnick
Series Editors: Liz and John Soars

OXFORD

CONTENTS

1 Education and learning

READING Good study habits

1 Discuss the questions with a partner.

1 What was your favourite and least favourite subject at school? Why?
2 When do you find it best to study? Why?

2 Look at *Texts A* and *B* on page 5 and answer the questions.

1 Which text is a quiz?
2 Which text looks more serious?
3 Which text is about studying effectively?

3 Look at the texts again. Answer the questions.

Text A: 1 How many questions are there?
　　　　 2 How many answers are there for each question?
　　　　 3 What does the second part of the text tell you?
Text B: 1 How many parts are there?
　　　　 2 Is there an introduction?
　　　　 3 Is there a conclusion?

4 Read *Text B* quickly. Answer the questions.

1 Which is better: a planned target or a vague commitment?
2 What two rewards are mentioned?
3 What two reasons are given for delaying starting work?
4 What is a more effective way of revising?

5 What different ways did you read the texts to answer the questions in …

1 exercise 2?　2 exercise 3?　3 exercise 4?　**Read Study Skill**

6 Complete the quiz and then answer these questions.

1 What is your learning style?　2 Do you agree with your result? Why (not)?

7 Look at the words in the table from *Text B*. Write the part of speech. Match the words with their meanings.

STUDY SKILL Effective reading (1)

Choose what to read, and how to read it to become an effective reader.

Survey the material to decide whether it is useful:

- Look at the title, headings, pictures, or graphs.
- Look at the style of the text and where it has come from.

Skim the text to see how the information is organized and to get a general idea:

- Read the title and any headings.
- Read the first sentence of a few paragraphs.

Scan the text to find specific pieces of information:

- Use what you learnt from surveying and skimming the text to locate the information you need.
- Move quickly through the text. Do not read every word.
- Stop when you come to the information you want.

word	part of speech	meaning
a crucial	adjective	1 producing a successful result
b effective		2 awake/able to concentrate
c vague		3 find (information) again
d incentive		4 frightening or worrying
e alert		5 something that encourages you
f put off		6 study hard in a short time
g daunting		7 extremely important
h worthwhile		8 delay doing something
i retrieve		9 not clear or definite
j cram		10 useful

A What is your learning style?

Answer the questions in our quick quiz to find out how you learn best!

1 Do you think you learn better by …
   A reading?   B listening to lectures?
2 How do you prefer to learn from lectures?
   A I like to make notes during the lecture.
   B I like to record the lecture and listen again.
3 When the teacher uses a new word, do you want to see it written …
   A immediately?   B later?
4 If you need to memorize something, e.g. a formula, a quotation, or a poem, do you …
   A write it out several times?
   B repeat it aloud to yourself and/or other people?
5 When you record new vocabulary, do you record the pronunciation?
   A Hardly ever   B Usually
6 Do you ever read aloud to yourself (in your own language or in English)?
   A Rarely   B Sometimes

Results

Mostly As

If you scored mostly As, you are a more visual learner. You prefer to see the written word. You learn by reading and writing. Visual learners often think in pictures. If you find a particular task or text difficult, look for sources that will suit your learning style, e.g. sources with illustrations, charts, tables, or videos.

Mixture As and Bs

If you scored mostly Bs, you are probably a more auditory learner. You prefer to learn by listening and speaking. Auditory learners often learn best from lectures, discussions, by reading aloud, and by listening to audio material.

Mixture As and Bs

If you scored a mixture of As and Bs, like most people you probably learn through a mixture of styles. Sometimes you may prefer to learn by reading, at other times by listening. Ask yourself which is the best style for the particular task you are doing.

(280 words)

B Becoming an effective student

Learning how to study effectively is an essential skill for students in any discipline. There are six areas which are **crucial** to developing good study habits. Work on these and you will become an **effective** student.

Targets

Always set a realistic work target. Don't try to do too much. For example, plan to read one chapter of a book each evening rather than think about reading the whole book over the weekend. This kind of detailed, planned target is more effective than a **vague** commitment. It is sometimes helpful to tell your friends about your plan. This is a good **incentive** to keep you on target because they will know if you fail!

Rewards

Develop a system of small rewards for your work. For example, stop for a cup of coffee or tea, or listen to a favourite piece of music after one hour's study. Rewarding yourself for keeping to your work plan will make you feel good about yourself.

Timing

Make sure you choose a suitable time to study, i.e. when it is quiet and when you are most **alert**. Try to make this a regular, time-tabled part of your day. If you plan to start work at a certain time, say 7pm, do not find reasons to **put off** getting started. You can watch a DVD later, and your emails are not urgent!

Quantity

A large task such as researching a new topic for an essay can be **daunting** – so daunting, in fact, that it can be difficult to sit down and make a start. Break the larger task down into several smaller ones. For example, make a list of questions that you will have to deal with in your essay, and then approach each question separately. This makes the work more manageable.

Notes and learning styles

The books you are studying won't always present information in a way that suits your learning style. It is, therefore, **worthwhile** spending time making notes and organizing them in a way that suits you best. It is also a good idea to keep your notebooks neat and well organized. This will make it much easier to **retrieve** information later.

Revision

Don't leave revision until the last moment. When you set your study targets, allow regular revision time. This is much more effective than trying to **cram** before an exam.

(395 words)

---

8 **Read Study Skill** Read *Text B* again. Write answers to the questions.

1 How does the writer think you can develop good study habits?
2 Why is it a good idea to tell other people about your work plans?
3 Why does the writer believe it is useful to reward yourself?
4 What makes one time to study better than another?
5 How can a large or complicated piece of work be made easier?
6 What is the main benefit of keeping good class or lecture notes?
7 How does the writer suggest you could improve your revision?

9 In your own studies, in which of the six areas in the article could you improve? How? Compare your answers with a partner.

STUDY SKILL Effective reading (2)

You will often need to understand the details in a text. This is **intensive reading**. To do this effectively:

- Think about why you are reading, and what you need from the text.
- Skim the text to get an overview.
- Underline words and phrases which occur frequently and are important to know.
- If a particular part of the text is more difficult, read it again, asking yourself questions about it.
- Look up any words you need to understand in a dictionary.

Education in the UK

10 Skim the text *The UK education system*. Which paragraph …

1 describes the school year?
2 gives an overview of education in the UK?
3 describes secondary education from 11 to 16?
4 describes primary education?
5 describes secondary education from 16 to 18?

11 **Read Study Skill** Underline the content words in sentences 1–3 from the text.

STUDY SKILL Effective reading (3)

You will have a large amount to read for your studies, so you need to be able to read quickly.

The first time you read a text intensively:

- Focus on content words (usually nouns, verbs, adjectives).

*It is **easy** to **read** this by **looking** at the **content words**.*

- Think about which parts of the text are relevant.

For further readings of the same text:

- Concentrate on parts of the text which are relevant.
- Read in sense groups of two or more words. Sense groups can be:
  subject + verb + object

*At the age of 16/**most students take exams**/in about ten different subjects.*
  phrases with a preposition

***At the age of 16**/most students take exams/**in about ten different subjects**.*

---

1 The school year runs from September to July and is usually divided into three terms of approximately 13 weeks each.
2 These schools are largely co-educational, that is, boys and girls attend together.
3 Most students go to large comprehensive schools which teach children of varying abilities.

12 Use the content words to answer the questions on education.

1 Are the education systems in the Republic of Ireland and Northern Ireland similar?
education system/Republic of Ireland/different/Northern Ireland
2 What schools do some 9-year-olds go to?
parts/England/children/leave/primary school/aged nine/go/middle school
3 How many young people go on to further education?
40%/young people/go/further education

13 Divide the first paragraph from the text into sense groups.
Read the paragraph aloud to a partner. Compare your paragraphs.

By law in the UK / all children between 5 and 16 years of age / must receive a full-time education. / The vast majority, over 90%, of these children attend state schools. The education systems in Wales, Northern Ireland, and England are similar, whereas the education system in Scotland differs in a number of ways. This description will generally refer to the English state system.

---

14 Which paragraphs in the text are relevant if you are only interested in …

1 primary education? 2 secondary education? 3 education in Scotland?

The UK education system

A By law in the UK, all children between 5 and 16 years of age must receive a full-time education. The vast majority, over 90%, of these children attend state schools. The education systems in Wales, Northern Ireland, and England are similar, whereas the education system in Scotland differs in a number of ways. This description will generally refer to the English state system.

B The school year runs from September to July and is usually divided into three terms of approximately 13 weeks each. Students attend school from about 9.00 am to 3.30 pm, Monday to Friday, with a morning break and a break for lunch. Some students eat lunch in the school cafeteria, but many bring food from home.

C Most children in England go to primary school from the age of 5 to 11. These schools are largely co-educational, that is, boys and girls attend together. All schools follow the National Curriculum. The core, or main subjects, are English, mathematics, and science. Other subjects include history, geography, physical education, music, and art. In Wales, the Welsh language is a subject in Welsh-speaking schools. In the same way, in Northern Ireland, the curriculum includes the Irish language in Irish-speaking schools.

D At the age of 11 students move to a secondary school. Most students go to large comprehensive schools which teach children of varying abilities. At the age of 16, most students take exams (GCSEs) in about ten different subjects. At this point, just under 50% leave school and start other training or work.

E Students who remain in education can choose to continue at their school for up to two years, or go to a special college. Wherever they study, students specialize in three or four subjects, and there are further exams at the age of 17 (AS Levels) and again at 18 (A Levels). Good results in these are required to go to university. (315 words)

LANGUAGE FOR WRITING Comparing and contrasting

1 Look at the underlined expressions in the sentences from the text on page 6. Do they show that things are similar or different?

> The education systems in Wales, Northern Ireland, and England are similar, <u>whereas</u> the education system in Scotland differs in a number of ways.
>
> In Wales, the Welsh language is a subject in Welsh-speaking schools. <u>In the same way</u>, in Northern Ireland, the curriculum includes the Irish language in Irish-speaking schools.

2 Underline other words and phrases in the sentences which show a similarity or a difference.

1 The school year in the UK runs from September to July. In Australia, on the other hand, students go to school from late January to December.
2 Both Sweden and France have a compulsory national curriculum.
3 Japanese schools are different from schools in many other countries in that they usually have an entrance exam.
4 Malaysian schools have two terms a year. In contrast, Australian schools have four terms.
5 School students all over the world are similar in that they have to take exams.

3 Add the words and phrases which you have underlined in exercise 2 to the correct part of the table. Make a note of the punctuation.

similar	different
In the same way, ...	..., whereas ...

4 Use a word or phrase from the table to complete the sentences.

1 _____ Wales _____ Ireland include their own language in the curriculum.
2 State and private schools _____ _____ _____ _____ all their students take school-leaving exams.
3 Northern Ireland and Wales have a similar education system to England. Scotland, _____ _____ _____ _____, has its own system.
4 In the UK, education is compulsory for children until the age of 16, _____ in Brazil children can leave school at 14.
5 Students in Japanese schools often eat school lunches. _____ _____ _____ _____, students in France also often eat in school.

5 Complete the sentences with your own ideas.

1 Schools and universities are similar in that _____.
2 Both boys and girls _____.
3 Literature is an arts subject. In contrast, _____.
4 English students take A Levels, whereas students in my country _____.
5 Primary school is different from _____ in that _____.

WRITING Education in Japan and England: a comparison

1 Write three things you remember about the UK education system. Are these things the same or different in your country? Discuss with a partner.

2 Look at the notes. Write a heading for each group of facts.

England	Japan	your country: _____
1 General information 1.1 compulsory for 5–16 year olds 1.2 90% + go to state schools	1 _____ 1.1 compulsory for 6–15 year olds 1.2 majority – state schools but some private (25%)	
2 _____ 2.1 September – July 2.2 3 terms – about 13 weeks each 2.3 Mon–Fri 9.00–3.30 pm 2.4 lunch break – cafeteria, packed lunches	2 _____ 2.1 April to March 2.2 3 terms – about 35 weeks a year 2.3 Mon–Fri 8.30–3.50 2.4 lunch break – most eat school food	
3 _____ 3.1 ages 5–11 3.2 co-educational 3.3 English, maths, science + others	3 Elementary school 3.1 ages 6–12 3.2 co-educational 3.3 Japanese, maths, science + others	
4 _____ 4.1 ages 11–16 and 17–18 4.2 comprehensive – all abilities	4 High school 4.1 junior high ages 12–15 4.2 senior high ages 15–18	
5 _____ 5.1 age 16 – GSCEs in 10 subjects 5.2 age 17 – AS Levels in 3 or 4 subjects 5.3 age 18 – A Levels in 3 subjects for university entrance	5 _____ 5.1 entrance exam to each school 5.2 entrance exam to each university	

3 Write two or three questions for each heading.

<u>General information</u>
1   When is school compulsory?
2   What percentage of students go to state schools?

4 Work with a partner. Answer your questions from exercise 3 about your country. Write your answers in note form in the table.

5 **Read Study Skill** Read the two long sentences from an essay comparing the education systems of Japan and England. Divide each sentence into two shorter ones.

> By law, Japanese children have to attend school from the age of 6 to 15, on the other hand, English children start compulsory school at the age of 5 and continue until they are 16.
>
> The Japanese and English education systems are similar in that it is necessary to take an exam to enter university however, Japan is different from England because each university sets its own entrance exam, whereas all English universities accept students with good A level results.

STUDY SKILL Checking your writing (1)

Being accurate is very important in academic and professional writing. Check your first draft for:
- sentence length. Are your sentences too long or short?
- word order, linking words
- words left out, e.g. articles, prepositions, and auxiliary verbs

---

6 Read the pairs of short sentences from the essay. Rewrite each pair to make one sentence, using words or phrases to show similarity or difference from *Language for Writing* on page 7.

> 1 The Japanese school year starts in April. The English school year starts in September.
> 2 English schools have three terms. Japanese schools have three terms.
> 3 Japanese students eat a school lunch. Many English students take food to school for lunch.

7 Read the paragraph. Find and correct …
1 two wrong uses of similarity and difference linking words and phrases
2 two missing prepositions
3 two examples of wrong word order

> The school systems in Japan and England are different in that students have to take exams. However, Japan each school can set entrance exams. In the same way, English schools do usually not have entrance exams. At the end of their time school, students in both countries have to exams take to enter university. There are places for everyone with the right qualifications, but very good grades are required to get into the best universities in both countries. Although there are a number of significant differences between the systems, both countries share a commitment to high quality education for their young people.

Writing a comparing and contrasting essay

8 Write an essay (150–200 words) comparing the education system in your country with **either** England **or** Japan. Use words and phrases from *Language for Writing* on page 7.

9 After you have written, check for sentence length, missing words, and the use of linking words and phrases.

VOCABULARY DEVELOPMENT Dictionary work

1 **Read Study Skill** Scan the entry for *dictionary*. Answer the questions.

> ### STUDY SKILL Using a dictionary (1)
>
> Choose a recent edition of an English–English dictionary. Look at the information about how to use the dictionary, which is usually at the beginning. Make sure you understand the symbols and abbreviations. Remember that each entry for a word usually has:
>
> - the pronunciation and stress
> - the part of speech
> - any irregular forms, e.g. plurals or past tense forms
> - definition(s)
> - example sentences

1 How many syllables are there in the word *dictionary*?
2 Which syllable has the main stress?
3 What part of speech is it?
4 What is the plural form?
5 How many meanings are given?

2 Scan the extract *lean* to *leasehold* from the *Oxford Student's Dictionary*. Answer the questions.

1 What part of speech is *leap*²?
2 How many syllables does the word *leasehold* have?
3 Where is the main stress on the adjective *leasehold*?
4 Find an adjective which means *thin*.
5 Find two uncountable nouns.
6 What are the past participles of the verb *lean*?
7 What are the past simple forms of the verb *learn*?

3 **Read Study Skill** Complete the sentences with the correct preposition. Use a dictionary to help.

> ### STUDY SKILL Using a dictionary (2)
>
> A dictionary entry will also help you use a word by giving:
>
> - any prepositions which collocate, e.g. *by* accident
> - verb type, e.g. transitive [T] (*I* **like music**); intransitive [I] (*He doesn't* **work**)
> - verb pattern, e.g. *let sb/sth* **do sth**; *allow sb* **to do sth**
>
> Always look at the example sentences. These will help you use the words accurately.

1 This master's degree consists _____ six modules.
2 There are many scholarships available _____ overseas students.
3 Education in most countries is funded mainly _____ the state.
4 The Internet is a good source _____ information.
5 If you wish to apply _____ a university, you should prepare your application carefully.

4 Check the underlined words and find the mistakes in the sentences. Use a dictionary to help.

1 The university <u>lets</u> students to use dictionaries in their exams.
2 Students are <u>encouraged</u> joining university societies.
3 Students are <u>expected</u> hand in their work on time.
4 Please <u>speak</u> your tutor if you have any problems.
5 Students usually <u>sit</u> on their exams in June.

---

dictionary 🔊 /'dɪkʃənri/ *noun* [C] (*pl.* **dictionaries**) **1** a book that contains a list of the words in a language in the order of the alphabet and that tells you what they mean, in the same or another language: *to look up a word in a dictionary* ◇ *a bilingual/monolingual dictionary* **2** a book that lists the words connected with a particular subject and tells you what they mean: *a dictionary of idioms* ◇ *a medical dictionary*

---

lean¹ 🔊 /liːn/ *verb* (*pt, pp* **leant** /lent/ or **leaned** /liːnd/) **1** [I] to move the top part of your body and head forwards, backwards or to the side: *He leaned across the table to pick up the phone.* ◇ *She leaned out of the window and waved.* ◇ *Just lean back and relax.* **2** [I] to be in a position that is not straight or UPRIGHT: *That wardrobe leans to the right.* **3** [I,T] ~ (sth) **against/on sth** to rest against sth so that it gives support; to put sth in this position: *She had to stop and lean on the gate.* ◇ *Please don't lean bicycles against this window.*

lean² /liːn/ *adj.* **1** (used about a person or animal) thin and in good health **2** (used about meat) having little or no fat **3** not producing much: *a lean harvest*

leap¹ /liːp/ *verb* [I] (*pt, pp* **leapt** /lept/ or **leaped** /liːpt/) **1** to jump high or a long way: *The horse leapt over the wall.* ◇ *A fish suddenly leapt out of the water.* ◇ *We all leapt into the air when they scored the goal.* ◇ (*figurative*) *Share prices leapt to a record high yesterday.* **2** to move quickly: *I looked at the clock and leapt out of bed.* ◇ *She leapt back when the pan caught fire.*
PHRV **leap at sth** to accept a chance or offer with enthusiasm: *She leapt at the chance to work in television.*

leap² /liːp/ *noun* [C] **1** a big jump: *He took* ***a flying leap*** *at the wall but didn't get over it.* ◇ (*figurative*) *My heart gave a leap when I heard the news.* **2** a sudden large change or increase in sth: *The development of penicillin was a great* ***leap forward*** *in the field of medicine.*

leapfrog /'liːpfrɒg/ *noun* [U] a children's game in which one person bends over and another person jumps over their back

'leap year *noun* [C] one year in every four, in which February has 29 days instead of 28

learn 🔊 /lɜːn/ *verb* (*pt, pp* **learnt** /lɜːnt/ or **learned** /lɜːnd/) **1** [I,T] ~ (sth) **(from sb/sth)** to get knowledge, a skill, etc. (from sb/sth): *I'm not very good at driving yet – I'm still learning.* ◇ *We're learning about China at school.* ◇ *Debbie is learning to play the piano.* ◇ *to learn a foreign language/a musical instrument* ◇ *Where did you learn how to swim?* **2** [I] ~ (of/about) sth to get some information about sth; to find out: *I was sorry to learn about your father's death.* **3** [T] (EDUCATION) to study sth so that you can repeat it from memory **4** [I] to understand or realize: *We should have learned by now that we can't rely on her.* ◇ *It's important to learn from your mistakes.*
IDM **learn your lesson** to understand what you must do/not do in the future because you have had an unpleasant experience

learned /'lɜːnɪd/ *adj.* having a lot of knowledge from studying; for people who have a lot of knowledge

learner /'lɜːnə(r)/ *noun* [C] a person who is learning: *a learner driver* ◇ *books for young learners*

learning /'lɜːnɪŋ/ *noun* [U] (EDUCATION) **1** the process of learning sth: *new methods of language learning* **2** knowledge that you get from studying

lease /liːs/ *noun* [C] (LAW) a legal agreement that allows you to use a building or land for a fixed period of time in return for rent: *The lease on the flat runs out/expires next year.* ▶ **lease** *verb* [T]: *They lease the land from a local farmer.* ◇ *Part of the building is leased out to tenants.* ▶ **leasing** *noun* [U]: *car leasing* ◇ *a leasing company*

leasehold /'liːshəʊld/ *adj.* (used about property or land) that you can pay to use for a limited period of time: *a leasehold property* ▶ **leasehold** *noun* [U] ↪ look at **freehold**

REVIEW

1 Would you skim, scan, or read intensively to …

1 find a word in a dictionary?
2 decide if you need to read an article in a journal?
3 get information from an article for an essay?
4 understand how a biological process such as photosynthesis works?
5 make notes about the education system in India?

2 Use the content words to write full sentences.

1 need   read   difficult   text   several   times
2 Japanese   students   go   school   seven   hours   day
3 typical   university   course   lasts   three   four   years
4 students   use   Internet   get   information

3 **Read Study Skill** Read the text. Find and correct …

1 three spelling mistakes
2 three punctuation mistakes
3 three grammar mistakes

> **STUDY SKILL** Checking your writing (2)
>
> Good academic writing should be accurate. Always check for correct:
> - punctuation
> - spelling
> - grammar (verb tenses, agreement, etc.)

Here to help!

Are you a new student. In your first few days at university you will need to register for your classes, and found out where and when they are held. You will also meet many new people, students lecturers, and other members of the university staff. you will certainly be give long lists of books that are required reading for your course, as well as a list of essays and other course asignments.

All of this can be very daunting and stressful. But don't worry, we are here to help you. **The Students' Advisory Group (SAG)** is avaliable to answer you questions, show you around the university, and to help with any other proplems.

Come to our office in Room 501, 5th floor, Central Building, or ask any student wearing a SAG badge. And good luck with your studies!

4 Look at the words in the box. Use a dictionary to answer the questions for each word.

chemistry   ability   compulsory   apply   tertiary   choose

1 What is the part of speech?
2 Where is the main stress?
3 What are the past forms of the verbs?
4 What are the plural forms of the nouns?

5 Add a word from exercise 4 in the correct form to the sentences.

1 Last year more students _____ to study sciences than in any previous year.

2 In some countries learning a foreign language is _____, whereas in other countries students can decide to study a language or not.

3 Comprehensive schools are schools which teach students of all _____.

4 More and more young people are going on to _____ education, either a university or some other educational establishment.

5 Last year 35% of our students _____ to university to study business management.

6 There are two basic types of _____: organic and inorganic.

2 Innovations in health and medicine

READING SKILLS Predicting content • Topic sentences • Avoiding plagiarism (1)
LANGUAGE FOR WRITING Rephrasing
WRITING SKILLS Developing a paragraph • Writing a paragraph
VOCABULARY DEVELOPMENT Recording vocabulary (1), (2), and (3)

READING A musical cure

1 Work with a partner. Where, when, and why do people listen to music? Brainstorm as many ideas as you can in two minutes.

2 ▐ Read Study Skill ▐ Look at the text on page 13. Answer the questions.

> ### STUDY SKILL Predicting content
>
> Predicting the content of a text will help you understand it.
> To predict the content, survey and skim the text (see Study Skill p4).

   1 Where could the text come from?
   2 What do the pictures show?
   3 Who is the text for?

     a musicians   b general readers   c medical specialists

3 Use the title of the text and the question words in the box to make questions.

> Where …?   How …?   What …?   Who …?

Where is music used as therapy?

4 Skim the text and find the answers to your questions in exercise 3.

5 ▐ Read Study Skill ▐ Read the text and underline the topic sentences in paragraphs 3–6.

> **1** <u>A recent study funded by the Wellcome Trust has investigated the connection between the use of music and the recovery of patients suffering from a variety of medical conditions.</u> The study has brought together musicians, health workers, and researchers to find evidence of the beneficial effects music has on health.

STUDY SKILL Topic sentences

Many paragraphs contain a topic sentence which gives the subject of the paragraph. The topic sentence is often the first sentence, but it can also be later in the paragraph.

6 Read the questions. Use the topic sentences to locate the answers to the questions.

   1 Is there any clear proof that music can heal? **Paragraph 6**
   2 For which diseases is music currently used?
   3 What effects does music have on people?
   4 Do we know how music therapy works?
   5 What effects does feeling good have on our health?

7 Scan the text and answer the questions in exercise 6.

8 Highlight the information which develops the topic sentences in paragraphs 3–6. Look at the example in paragraph 2 first.

Music used as a healing therapy

1 A recent study funded by the Wellcome Trust has investigated the connection between the use of music and the recovery of patients suffering from a variety of medical conditions. The study has brought together musicians, health workers, and researchers to find evidence of the beneficial effects music has on health.

2 <u>Music has long been used to treat patients suffering from different problems</u>. In 400 BCE, its healing properties were documented by the ancient Greeks. More recently, in both world wars in the last century, medical workers used music therapy with people suffering from trauma. Currently, it is used as a treatment for many diseases, such as cancer and Alzheimer's disease, and it has also been used with patients with long-term pain and learning disabilities.

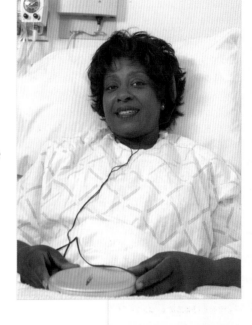

3 There is growing evidence that music can cause physical changes to the body which can improve our health. In the Wellcome Trust study, which took place over three years at the Chelsea and Westminster hospital in London, patients were asked to listen to musical performances. As a result, it was found that stress levels were significantly reduced, recovery times were improved, and fewer drugs were needed.

4 These very positive results are partly due to general well-being. It is already accepted that when people feel happy and have a positive approach to life, they are more likely to feel better and recover from disease quickly. Music increases this feeling of joy and adds to the recovery process.

5 However, not all these benefits can be attributed to an increase in general well-being. Music has other effects which have not yet been understood. According to Professor Robertson, a scientist and musician, some effects of music are mysterious and are, therefore, being investigated further. It has been suggested that the sounds and rhythms of music help stimulate the brain and send electrical messages to the muscles and limbs.

6 Science, however, demands facts and hard evidence. Many in the medical profession have not yet recognized the healing benefits of music, since reports have been based mainly on anecdotal evidence. These new studies could provide proof to medical practitioners that music is a suitable treatment for many conditions. One day doctors may even 'prescribe' music, but that could be a long time in the future.

(383 words)

A new vaccine

9 Read the title of the article from a medical journal. What is the article about? Compare your ideas with a partner.

10 Use the key words in the box to predict what each paragraph is about. Use a dictionary if necessary.

11 Skim the article. Were your predictions correct?

A	vaccine cured
B	involved trials early stages advanced stages spread
C	stimulates immune system cells harmful
D	further studies

Promising results from cancer study

A A new experimental vaccine has shown promising results in the fight against lung cancer. In a small Texas-based study, a vaccine developed by scientists at Baylor University Medical Centre in Dallas, USA cured lung cancer in some patients and slowed the progress of the disease in others.

B Researchers have reported encouraging findings from this small study. Forty-three patients suffering from lung cancer were involved in these trials. Ten of these patients were in the early stages and thirty-three in the advanced stages of the disease. They were injected with the vaccine every two weeks for three months, and were carefully monitored for three years. In three of the patients in the advanced stages of cancer, the disease disappeared and in the others, it did not spread for five to twenty-four months. However, no great difference was seen in the patients in the early stages of the illness.

C This new vaccine uses the patient's own immune system. It is made specifically for each patient and is injected into the arm or leg. It stimulates the body's immune system, which then recognizes that the cancer cells are harmful, and attacks and destroys them.

D The vaccine could be effective against other forms of cancer. It offers great hope for the treatment of cancer in general, although further studies are needed before such treatment can be widely used.

(232 words)

Deakin, F. P. (2007). Promising results from cancer study. *New Medical Journal, 32.*

---

12 Scan the article. Are the statements true (**T**) or false (**F**)?

1 The investigation cured all of the participants in the trial.
2 About forty people participated in the study.
3 Patients in the early stages of the disease recovered more quickly.
4 Every patient was given the same vaccine.
5 The vaccine activates the immune system.
6 This treatment may be useful for treating other cancers.

13 Read the summary of the article. How is it different from the original? Discuss your answers with a partner.

> A group of US researchers has carried out trials of a new vaccine which is effective against lung cancer. Although the study was limited to fewer than fifty people, the results were very promising. Some of the patients at an advanced stage of the disease were cured. Each patient in the trial had their own vaccine which activated their body's immune system and enabled it to fight the cancer. It is hoped that other forms of cancer can be cured in a similar way.

14 **Read Study Skill** Read the summary again. Match the highlighted parts of the summary with parts of the text.

A group of US researchers = scientists at Baylor University Medical Centre in Dallas, USA

STUDY SKILL
Avoiding plagiarism (1)

Plagiarism is copying someone's work, or using someone's ideas and pretending they are your own. Do not copy directly from a text, but rephrase by changing:

- the vocabulary (using synonyms or phrases with a similar meaning)
- the sentence structure and grammar

NOTE You must always credit the source when you use another person's ideas, opinions, facts, and graphics, even if you paraphrase their words.

LANGUAGE FOR WRITING Rephrasing

1 Look at the sentences below from the summary on page 14. Replace the underlined words with a suitable synonym or near synonym from the box.

> tests   scientists   encouraging   illness
> research   recovered   findings   conducted

1 A group of US <u>researchers</u> has <u>carried out</u> <u>trials</u> on a new vaccine.
2 Although the <u>study</u> was limited to fewer than fifty people, the <u>results</u> were very <u>promising</u>.
3 Some of the patients at an advanced stage of the <u>disease</u> <u>were cured</u>.

2 Rewrite each sentence from exercise 1, using the synonyms.

A group of US scientists has conducted tests on a new vaccine.

3 Read the rules. Rewrite the sentences in the correct form of the passive.

> **RULES** The passive voice
>
> The passive voice is used when it not important *who* or *what* does an action.
> It is formed by the verb *to be* in the correct tense + the past participle.
> *The vaccine **is injected** into the arm or leg.*
> *The patients **were injected** with the vaccine.*
> In most passive sentences, *by* and the agent (the subject of the active sentence) are omitted because the agent is obvious or not necessary.
> *The patients were carefully monitored for three years ~~by doctors~~.*
> NOTE An academic text will usually have a mixture of active and passive sentences.

1 Pharmaceutical companies are constantly developing new drugs.

New drugs are constantly being developed by pharmaceutical companies.

2 The government provided the funding for the study.
3 Doctors have used alternative therapies for many years.
4 Scientists usually test their theories in the laboratory.
5 The researchers will publish their findings next month.

4 Find the words or phrases which are synonyms in the pairs of sentences.

After only six months the (team's) (research) was (completed.)

The (group's) (study) was (finished) after only six months.

1 a The main causes of acute asthma attacks are common cold viruses.
  b Common cold viruses are the principal causes of severe asthma attacks.
2 a Scientists use radiation to investigate details of tiny structures.
  b Scientists use radiation to study details of very small structures.
3 a A short ten-minute walk every day can be beneficial to your health.
  b Walking for ten minutes daily can benefit your health.

5 Rephrase the sentences, using synonyms and the passive voice where appropriate.

1 We need proof that the medicine works.
2 They will build a huge medical centre in the near future.
3 An unhealthy lifestyle can be the cause of many diseases.
4 The organizers cancelled the talk because the speaker was ill.

WRITING Keeping healthy

1 Work with a partner. Discuss the questions.

   1 How often should you see a doctor?
   2 How do you keep healthy?
   3 What is meant by a balanced diet?

2 **Read Study Skill** Read paragraph A and look at the underlined topic sentence. Read paragraphs B and C and write a topic sentence for each paragraph. Compare your sentences with a partner.

Focus on Health

A Exercise

There are a few things to remember when you take exercise. Warm up properly before starting, choose comfortable loose-fitting clothing, and stop if you don't feel well. Take some rest if you need it, and remember that exercise should be fun!

B Dehydration

_____. Not drinking enough water causes dryness of the mouth, headaches, and dizziness as well as feelings of confusion. You should drink at least one litre of water a day, and more if you are exercising, or in hot weather. Dehydration is common in very young children, people who over-exercise, older people if the weather is very hot, and those suffering from diabetes.

C Diet

_____. The body requires all of the important food groups: fats, carbohydrates, proteins, fibre, and vitamins and minerals. You should not omit any of these groups from your diet completely, but maintain a sensible balance of all five. Choose a diet which is high in fruit and vegetables and low in fats and sugar.

3 Read the topic sentences in the box. Use sentences a–f to develop the topic sentences into a paragraph. Write out each paragraph in full.

> 1 We should all eat five portions of fruit and vegetables a day, according to nutritionists.
> 2 Obesity is a growing problem all over the world.

a It has been proved that eating regular amounts of fresh fruit and vegetables reduces the risk of developing serious diseases.
b In some developed countries, over 50% of the population is overweight.
c This is in part due to an unhealthy diet, but also to lack of exercise.
d It is easy to follow these guidelines by having fruit juice for breakfast and vegetables with your main course at lunch, followed by a piece of fruit for dessert.
e There is also growing concern over the number of young people who suffer from weight problems.
f If you then include salad or more vegetables with your evening meal, you will soon reach the target five portions.

fats
carbohydrates
fibre
proteins
vitamins and minerals

4 Write three body sentences for this topic sentence. Compare your sentences with a partner.

The weather can affect how people feel.

5 Match final sentences 1–3 with paragraphs A–C.

1 ☐ Their findings are published in the journal *Nature*.
2 ☐ These cells then heal the damage at the cut.
3 ☐ As a result, the healing process is accelerated.

The healing power of electricity Focus on Science

A Scientists have discovered how the body uses electricity to heal cuts. When a person's skin is cut, an electrical signal forms at the edge of the wound and it remains there until the wound heals. This electrical signal stimulates special skin cells to move to the wound. _____.

B The effects of the electrical charge are very slow. The skin cells move at a speed of fifty micrometres an hour, which is approximately one millimetre a day. However, experiments have shown that the mechanism can be speeded up by fifty per cent. _____.

C In fact, this is a rediscovery of an old medical observation. In the mid-1880s, a German scientist measured the electrical charge across a wound in his arm. At that time it was not considered to be an important discovery. The researchers in Scotland have now confirmed his observations and explained the process behind it. _____.

6 Write a final sentence for these two paragraphs.

Antibiotics

One of the greatest scientific advances of the last century was the discovery of antibiotics. Antibiotics are drugs which kill or stop the growth of bacteria. The first modern antibiotic was penicillin. Since its discovery, many more antibiotics have been discovered or manufactured, and have proved essential in the fight against some diseases. However, if they are overused or used wrongly, they become ineffective. _____.

Back pain

Many people suffer from back pain. It is said that four out of five adults will suffer from back pain at some time in their lives. There are many causes and types of back pain, and there are various treatments. Previously the treatment for back pain was bed rest, but these days many doctors recommend light exercise. _____.

Writing a paragraph

7 Write a paragraph (80–100 words) about each of the topics. Include a topic sentence, several body sentences, and a concluding sentence.

- Vaccinations
- The prevention of diseases

VOCABULARY DEVELOPMENT Recording vocabulary

1 Read Study Skill Which of the words would be more useful to …

1 a literature student? 2 a medical student? 3 all students?

curriculum	heal	data	novel	therapy	analyse	grading
immune	define	course	vaccine	lecture	disease	author

2 Read Study Skill Look at the vocabulary records and answer the questions.

1 Which words have been recorded for active use?
2 Which words have been recorded for understanding only?

STUDY SKILL Recording vocabulary (2)

What you record about a word depends on how you will use it. If you only need to **understand** the word, record:

- the pronunciation
- a definition and/or translation

If there is a word which you want to **use** in your own work, record:

- the pronunciation
- the part of speech
- any irregular forms
- associated prepositions or verb patterns
- an example sentence
- a definition and/or translation

3 Read Study Skill Which methods are used to record the vocabulary in 1–3 opposite?

STUDY SKILL Recording vocabulary (3)

It is important that you can remember vocabulary and find it again. Choose a suitable method to record it effectively. For example:

- according to topic
- as a mind map
- as a group of words with similar meanings

4 Divide the vocabulary in the box into three groups. Choose a suitable method to record each group.

scientists	geneticists	encouraging	proteins	physicists
food	favourable	fats	vitamins	minerals	biologists
promising	sugars	positive	chemists	carbohydrates

STUDY SKILL Recording vocabulary (1)

When you read, you will come across many new words. It is not possible or useful to record them all. Choose words which:

- are related to your academic studies
- are key words in the text
- will be useful when you write

Vocabulary records

- **prestigious** /preˈstɪdʒəs/ – *having a good reputation, respected*

- **suffer (from sth)** /ˈsʌfə(r)/ *verb* **[I,T]** – *to experience something unpleasant such as pain, disease, etc.*
  e.g. Barbara suffered a heart attack last year.
  Syn: experience

- **intake** /ˈɪnteɪk/ – *the process of taking food, drink, etc. into your body*

- **cut** /kʌt/ *noun* – *a hole or wound made with something sharp*
  e.g. He had a cut on his head.

1 Vocabulary of health & medicine

- **to prescribe medicine** – *to say what treatment or medicine sb should have*

- **treatment** *noun*, **to treat** *verb* – *to use medical care to make sb better*

- **to suffer from a disease/condition/illness**

2

3 a study/research/an investigation/a project/a survey

REVIEW

1 Survey the text and title and answer the questions.

1 Where could the text come from? 3 What do the pictures show?
2 Who is it written for? 4 What is it about?

2 Skim the text and match topic sentences 1–3 with paragraphs A–C.

1 ☐ AMD occurs when a region at the back of the eye starts to deteriorate.
2 ☐ Although there is currently only a cure for one type of AMD, diet and the increased consumption of certain vegetables appear to lower the risk of developing other forms of the disease.
3 ☐ Brightly-coloured vegetables can help protect your sight.

Do carrots help you see in the dark?

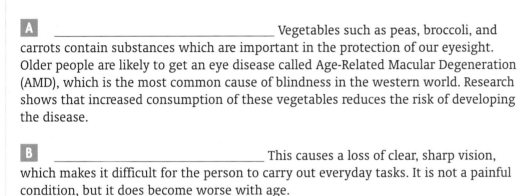

A _____ Vegetables such as peas, broccoli, and carrots contain substances which are important in the protection of our eyesight. Older people are likely to get an eye disease called Age-Related Macular Degeneration (AMD), which is the most common cause of blindness in the western world. Research shows that increased consumption of these vegetables reduces the risk of developing the disease.

B _____ This causes a loss of clear, sharp vision, which makes it difficult for the person to carry out everyday tasks. It is not a painful condition, but it does become worse with age.

C _____ Dr Suzen Moeller led a research group which studied a group of women between the ages of 50 and 79 at Wisconsin University, in the USA. The women's consumption of coloured vegetables was monitored over 15 years. It was concluded that women under 75 who have a high intake of these vegetables are less likely to develop the eye condition. It would seem that there is some truth in the saying that carrots are good for our eyes.

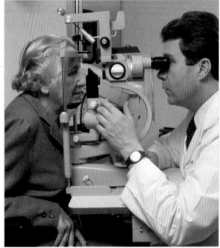

3 Read the text again and answer the questions.

1 Which people are most affected by AMD?
2 How does eating vegetables affect your chances of getting AMD?
3 What effect does AMD have on eyes?
4 How was the study carried out?

4 Rephrase the sentences in your own words.

1 Increased consumption of these vegetables reduces the risk of developing the disease.
2 Dr Suzen Moeller led a research group.
3 The women's consumption of coloured vegetables was monitored over 15 years.
4 Women under 75 who have a high intake of these vegetables are less likely to develop the eye condition.

5 Write a paragraph (80–100 words) about one of the topics.

• Diet and health   • A common illness

6 Choose ten words or phrases from Unit 2. Record five of them for active use and five for understanding only.

3 Urban planning

READING SKILLS Paragraph purpose • Text cohesion
RESEARCH Using reference material • Searching the Internet efficiently (1) and (2)
WRITING SKILLS Selecting information • Prioritizing • Brainstorming • Writing a persuasive article
VOCABULARY DEVELOPMENT Collocations (1)

READING A model of good urban planning

1 Work with a partner. Discuss the questions.

1 What changes have there been to your city in the last ten years?
2 Have these changes improved your city or not?

2 Survey the text on page 21 and the two pictures. Answer the questions.

1 Is the text from a newspaper or a professional journal?
2 What do the pictures show?
3 Which city is it about?

3 Skim the text. Will it be useful to research topics 1–4?

1 urban planning in Brazil
2 urban planning in Japan
3 Alfred Agache and his work
4 Curitiba's influence on urban planning

4 Scan the text and answer the questions.

1 Where is Curitiba?
2 When did the city employ the French architect?
3 What was the population of Curitiba in the 1980s?
4 Does the writer believe Curitiba is a good model of urban planning?

5 | Read Study Skill | Read the text again carefully. Match paragraphs A–H with their purpose 1–5.

1 ☐ evaluates the importance of the Curitiba model
2 ☐ ☐ ☐ ☐ describe developments
3 ☐ describes the current situation
4 ☐ describes the problem
5 ☐ states the purpose of the text

6 | Read Study Skill | Underline the language in the text which shows continuity between paragraphs A–G.

7 Match the paragraphs with the ways of showing continuity.

paragraph	linked by
a **3** A–B	1 rephrasing key words,
b ☐ B–C	e.g. integrate/integrated,
c ☐ C–D	city planning/urban design
d ☐ D–E	2 maintaining the subject 'good transportation'
e ☐ E–F	3 a backward reference
f ☐ F–G	4 a question
	5 repeating the key word 'Agache'
	6 a forward reference

Lessons from Curitiba

A This review will argue that Curitiba, in southern Brazil, is an important model of good urban planning. Urban planning deals with the physical, economic, and social development of cities. Today, urban populations are increasing rapidly, and growing cities are putting enormous pressure on the environment. For this reason, the type of urban planning found in Curitiba is more important than ever.

B As stated in the introduction, Curitiba is a fine example of how urban planning can work. This has not always been the case, however. At one time, Curitiba faced the same problems as many other cities all over the world, namely overcrowding, pollution, and an increased demand for services, transport, and housing. How, then, did Curitiba address these problems?

C By the 1940s the population of Curitiba had grown to about 150,000, as immigrants from countries such as Japan, Syria, and Lebanon came to work in agriculture and industry. These people needed both housing and transportation. Curitiba's leaders realized that it was not sensible to deal with these problems separately. Consequently, they employed a French planner and architect, Alfred Agache, to find an overall solution.

D Agache studied all aspects of the problem. He designed a scheme which gave priority to public services such as sanitation and public transport. At the same time, the scheme included centres which helped both community life and commerce to develop, and reduced traffic congestion. This was the first scheme to address several problems of growing cities at the same time. Unfortunately, some parts of his plan were not completed. The result, as described below, was that his scheme only served Curitiba for another 20 years.

E By the 1960s the population of Curitiba had grown to about 430,000 inhabitants, so the city had to rethink its needs. In order to do this, the mayor put together a team of architects and town planners led by Jaime Lerner. This team produced the Curitiba Master Plan. This consisted of taking Agache's original plan and adding wide, high-speed roads which crossed the smaller streets. Their proposals also included plans to minimize urban growth, reduce city-centre traffic, and preserve the city's historic district. It is clear that the Curitiba Master Plan was one of the first attempts to integrate all aspects of city planning.

F This integrated approach to urban design was maintained throughout the 1980s as Curitiba's population grew to almost one million inhabitants. Environmental facilities were added, such as a recycling programme for household waste, and parks and 'green' spaces were protected from development. However, good transportation remained central to the planning.

G Good transportation still remains a priority, together with the need for jobs. A growing population needs employment, so business parks and centres have been added to encourage new small businesses. All these challenges will continue as the population of Curitiba increases, but its city planners are continually searching for solutions to the problems.

H It is apparent that, as an increasing number of people move into cities, the challenges for urban planners will also grow. Many other cities are looking to Curitiba for answers. Its planners have been courageous and innovative, and have always put the city's inhabitants at the centre of their designs. Other city planners could benefit greatly from this experience.

(540 words)

8 Read the text again. Answer the questions.

1 What three aspects of development does urban planning deal with?
2 What problems do many cities face?
3 What was the main cause of the increase in Curitiba's population before the 1940s?
4 In what ways was Agache's approach different?
5 What happened to Agache's plan?
6 What did the Curitiba Master Plan do?
7 What was new about the approach to planning in the 1980s?
8 What is new about the approach to planning now?
9 What is the writer's opinion of the Curitiba experience of urban planning?

A new capital

A Dr Doxiadis and his colleagues looked at the various locations. They then produced a report suggesting two possible areas: one just outside Karachi and the other to the north of Rawalpindi. Both locations had advantages as well as disadvantages. Which site was it to be?

B Each of these three sections had a different role. Islamabad would act as the nation's capital and would serve its administrative and cultural needs, whereas Rawalpindi would remain the regional centre with industry and commerce. The third piece of the plan, the national park, was planned to provide space for education, recreation, and agriculture.

C The choice between these two options was made after consideration of many factors, such as transportation, the availability of water, economic factors, and factors of national interest. Finally, the site north of Rawalpindi was chosen and on the 24th February 1960, the new capital was given the name of 'Islamabad' and a master plan was drawn up. This master plan divided the area into three different sections: Islamabad itself, neighbouring Rawalpindi, and the national park.

D Rather than try to overcome these drawbacks, the government decided to create a new capital city. In 1959, a commission was established to investigate the possible locations of this new city. The advisor appointed to the commission was Dr Doxiadis, a famous architect and city planner.

E This article describes the background to the choice and development of Islamabad as the modern capital of Pakistan. When the new state of Pakistan was founded in 1947, Karachi acted as the capital city. However, it was difficult for Karachi to remain in this role due to a number of drawbacks such as the climate and the state of the existing buildings.

F Today Islamabad is a thriving city of about one million people. It offers a healthy climate, a pollution-free atmosphere, plenty of water, and many green spaces. It has wide, tree-lined streets, elegant public buildings, and well-organized bazaars and shopping centres. The new capital is a superb example of good urban planning.

(339 words)

9 Look at the text *A new capital*. The paragraphs are in the wrong order. Find the first paragraph and answer the questions.

1 Which country's capital city is discussed?
2 Which city was the old capital?
3 What city is the new capital?

10 Skim the other paragraphs and put them in the correct order. What language in the text helped you?

11 Scan the text to correct the factual errors in the sentences.

1 The country of Pakistan was created in 1948.
2 Dr Doxiadis was made leader of the commission.
3 The initial report described three places which could be used for the new capital.
4 The master plan split the new area into four sections.
5 Karachi was to maintain its role as the regional centre.
6 The capital is no longer doing well.

RESEARCH Finding information

1 [Read Study Skill] Match the words to their (near) synonyms.

1 **g** scheme   a factories
2 ☐ population   b business
3 ☐ agriculture   c city planning
4 ☐ commerce   d farming
5 ☐ employment   e jobs
6 ☐ household waste   f inhabitants
7 ☐ industry   g plan
8 ☐ urban design   h rubbish

STUDY SKILL Using reference material

If you cannot find a topic in a reference book or index, look under other related words to search for that topic. For example:
- (near) synonyms, e.g. *scheme / plan*
- more general or topic words, e.g. *biology / science*

2 Put the words in the box under the correct topic in the table.

bridges	biologist	hospital	museum	·physicist	post office
roads	diploma	sanitation	seminar	chemist	curriculum

infrastructure	scientists	public buildings	education
bridges			

3 [Read Study Skill] What kind of Internet site would you use to find information on 1–5?

1 modern architecture in Dubai
2 the designer of New Delhi
3 architecture
4 the date Alfred Agache was born
5 the work of Dr Doxiadis

STUDY SKILL Searching the Internet efficiently (1)

Choose an appropriate Internet site.
- For general information, e.g. *the history of Pakistan*, use a **subject directory** such as http://bubl.ac.uk/ or http://www.rdn.ac.uk/
- For more specific information, e.g. *urban planning in Indonesia*, use a **search engine** such as www.google.com or www.yahoo.com
- To check a fact, e.g. *the date of the independence of India*, use an **online encyclopaedia** such as www.bartleby.com

On some search engines, such as http://uk.ask.com you can ask direct questions, e.g. *Who designed Canberra?*

4 [Read Study Skill] What key words and symbols would you use to find information on 1–5?

1 the development of urban recycling schemes   *"urban recycling"*
2 the design and construction of Canberra, the capital of Australia
3 the earliest cities in Asia
4 the history of the city of Istanbul
5 famous architects (not American)

STUDY SKILL Searching the Internet efficiently (2)

Before doing research on the Internet, plan what and how you are going to search. Ask:
- What is my search topic?
- What are the key words or phrases? Write synonyms of the key words.

Use quotation marks for phrases. For example:

If you search *urban planning*, you will find sites with the words *urban* and *planning*. These words might not be connected.

If you search *"urban planning"*, you will find sites which have these words together.

To make your search more specific:
- Use + or AND to find information together, e.g. "urban planning" +Brazil.
- Use - or NOT to remove information you do not need, e.g. if you want information on urban planning but not in Europe, search *"urban planning" -Europe*.

WRITING An international trade fair

1 Three cities are competing to be the venue for an international trade fair to be held next summer. You are planning to write an article for a national magazine to persuade the readers that one of the cities, Urbania, is the best choice. Organize the information about Urbania into categories.

transportation	location	facilities	weather	trade & industry
1 an international airport 20km away				

Urbania

1   an international airport 20km away
2   a good network of roads to other parts of the country
3   several top-quality restaurants
4   doesn't usually rain in the summer
5   only 30 minutes away from capital city
6   average summer temperature is $24^{0}C$
7   a 20-hectare site ready for re-development
8   a mountain range about 5km away
9   hotel accommodation for 20,000 visitors
10   the centre for gold marketing and jewellery making
11   an excellent public transport system
12   a world famous computer manufacturer based in the city
13   only 10km from two international borders
14   a very low level of air pollution because of coastal winds
15   many private cars
16   snows heavily in the winter
17   famous for its boat-building industry
18   lots of shops
19   on the coast
20   a university

A trade fair

2 Go through the notes about Urbania. Cross out one piece of information in each category which is not relevant to the report. Compare your list with a partner. `Read Study Skill`

3 Look at categories a–e. In your opinion, which two are the most important, and why? Compare your answers with a partner. `Read Study Skill`

a   transportation
b   location
c   facilities
d   weather
e   trade & industry

4 Look at the information in each of the categories in exercise 1.
Number the information for each category in order of importance.

an excellent public transport system	**(2)**
a good network of roads to other parts of the country	**(3)**
an international airport 20km away	**(1)**

5 Link the information and write a short paragraph for each category.

> *Visitors can get to Urbania very easily because the international airport is only 20 kilometres away. When they are in the city, they can travel around quickly as there is an excellent public transport system. Furthermore, visitors can get to other parts of the country because Urbania has a good network of roads.*

6 Read the introduction to an article about Urbania. Add your own paragraphs from exercise 5. Link each paragraph to the next.

Why Urbania should hold the international trade fair

This article will demonstrate that Urbania is the best choice to hold the trade fair. It has excellent transport, is in a perfect location, and has first-class facilities. It also has important businesses and industries.

Writing a persuasive article

7 **Read Study Skill** Work with a partner. In five minutes, brainstorm information about your city. Organize the information into categories.

> **STUDY SKILL** Brainstorming
>
> Before writing, **brainstorm** for ideas:
> - Set a time for brainstorming, e.g. five or ten minutes.
> - Quickly write down everything you can about the topic in that time.
> - Don't worry about what is more or less important.
> - At the end of the time read, organize, select, and prioritize your notes.

transportation	location	facilities	weather	trade & industry

8 Your city would like to hold **one** of the events below. Decide which information from exercise 7 is relevant for this event.

- an international sporting event
- an international conference on university education
- a national marathon
- a national cultural event

9 Write an article (200–250 words) for a magazine, saying why your city should hold this event.

VOCABULARY DEVELOPMENT Collocations (1)

1 [Read Study Skill] Underline the collocations in the sentences.

STUDY SKILL Collocations (1)

Collocation are words which frequently appear together. Recognizing these collocations helps you understand a text better and improve your reading speed. If you use them in your writing, it will sound more natural.

Some common collocations are formed by:

- adjectives and nouns, e.g. *urban planning*
- verbs and nouns, e.g. *do research*

Always record these words together.

---

1 Curitiba is a model of good <u>urban planning</u>.
2 Good transportation is a high priority.
3 The government has announced that it will invest more money in public services.
4 The new highway will reduce traffic congestion around the city.
5 Before developing the city centre, the planners had to consider all the economic factors.
6 It is in everyone's best interests if planners consider the social effects of their schemes.

2 Choose the correct adjective and noun collocation. Use a dictionary to help.

1 _____ traffic
  a heavy   b big   c large
2 _____ estimate
  a approximate   b rough   c general
3 _____ economy
  a earthly   b universal   c global

Rush hour in Mexico City

3 Underline the noun which collocates with the verbs in bold.

1 Curitiba **faced** the same problems as other cities.
2 They **drew up** a radical new plan to improve traffic flow in the city.
3 Chemistry students often have to **do** experiments in a laboratory.
4 It is useful to **brainstorm** ideas before writing an essay.
5 The university staff **hold** a planning meeting before each academic year commences.
6 There is not enough room in the university library for the students. The library committee urgently need to **find** a solution to this problem.

4 Complete the sentences with a noun from the box.

> instructions   notes   problem   progress
> recommendations   report   survey

1 Many cities have to address the _____ of overcrowding.
2 When they finish doing the _____, the architects are expected to make many _____.
3 Please follow the _____ carefully.
4 If you review your _____ regularly, it will help you make better _____.
5 You need to write your _____ before the end of the month.

REVIEW

1 Look at the jumbled paragraphs from an essay on the history of urban planning. Read the paragraphs and put them into the correct order.

The history of urban planning

Harappa

A Similarly, in the first millennium BCE, the ancient Greeks were laying out their cities in an organized and regular manner. Alexandria and Miletus are two of the most famous examples of this urban planning. These cities also provided their inhabitants with public facilities such as market places and fresh water supplies.

B Islamic cities too provided their citizens with public facilities. They are further credited with developing a totally new idea of urban planning known as zoning. This is a system where different areas of a city are assigned different functions, such as religious, administrative, or commercial. The idea of zoning spread to many parts of Europe.

C There is evidence of deliberate planning as far back as the third millennium BCE in the Indus Valley. In the city of Harappa, now in modern Pakistan, there were water tanks and a system of urban sanitation, and the streets were paved and laid out in a regular grid.

D Urban planning is not a recent invention. People have designed their settlements from the earliest times. Despite differences based on geography, culture, and the needs of the population, the various planners had many things in common, as this essay will describe.

2 Complete the sentences using a verb from the box in its correct form.

> address   do   hold   make

1 The director will _____ a planning meeting on Monday.

2 The Olympic Games are _____ every four years.

3 The chancellor of the university is _____ the new students in the main hall at the moment.

4 It is important to _____ people properly in order not to offend them.

5 Students are asked not to _____ a noise if they leave before the end of the examination.

6 Building a road around the city will _____ a difference to traffic congestion.

7 Please _____ exercise 3 in pairs.

8 Next semester I am _____ a course in translation.

3 Use a dictionary to find other nouns which collocate with the verbs in the box in exercise 2.

4 Do an Internet search to answer the questions.
1 Who designed Brasilia?
2 What is the current population of Curitiba?
3 Which are the three largest cities in the world (by population) outside China and India?
4 Why was Canberra chosen as the location of Australia's capital city?

4 Water, food, and energy

READING SKILLS Finding information from more than one source • Identifying language for rephrasing and giving examples
LANGUAGE FOR WRITING Introductions and conclusions • Rephrasing and giving examples
WRITING SKILLS Introductions • Developing a thesis statement • Conclusions
Checking your writing (3) • Writing to describe and explain
VOCABULARY DEVELOPMENT Compound nouns • Compound adjectives

READING Water, water, everywhere

1 Discuss the statements.

- 'Water just comes out of a tap. I don't think about where it comes from.'
- 'Bottled water is good for you.'
- 'Water is more valuable than oil.'

2 Survey *Texts A* and *B* on page 29. Where could they come from? Who are they written for?

3 Scan the texts. What do the numbers in the box refer to?

70%	98%	1972	300 billion	25%	32,000	2.7 billion	150

4  **Read Study Skill** Look at questions 1–10. Read *Text A* and underline any information which answers the questions.

> ### STUDY SKILL
> ### Finding information from more than one source
>
> You will often have to read two or more texts about the same subject. The information you need will depend on the task.
> - Read the first text and underline the information you need.
> - Read the second text and underline any new or different information which is relevant.
> - Make notes from the information you have underlined.

1 What is desalination?
2 What is removed during desalination?
3 Which two methods are used in desalination?
4 Name three countries which use desalination.
5 When was desalination first used in China?
6 How have the Chinese made the process of desalination more efficient?
7 When was desalination first used in the UAE?
8 Why is there a water shortage in some countries with adequate rainfall?
9 How can water be managed more efficiently?
10 How can the problems of water be solved in the future?

5 Read *Text B* and underline any information which you could not find in *Text A* or which is different.

6 Make notes to answer the questions, using the information you have underlined in both texts.

A World of water

Water is essential to life and we depend on it, yet many people take water for granted. As the population of the world increases, and with it the demand for water, there is growing concern that our water supplies will not prove adequate. In areas near the coast, an obvious solution to this problem is to find ways of utilizing the abundant supply of water from the sea.

Water covers 70% of the surface of the earth, but 98% of this is undrinkable salt water. However, for centuries man has experimented with different methods of converting salt water into fresh water in a process called desalination, whereby salt and contaminants are removed from the water. The challenge, nowadays, is to do this on a much larger scale.

One place which has used desalination for many years is the United Arab Emirates. It installed the first desalination plants in 1972, and nowadays most of the drinking water in the country is supplied by this process. New filtration systems have been developed to replace the traditional methods, which used a heating process. Another example is Saudi Arabia, whose desalination plants produce almost 25% of the world's desalinated water. One of the largest plants in the world has been constructed there, producing 300 billion litres annually.

China, with its rapid industrial growth, has also experienced an increased demand for water as well as energy. To overcome the shortage of both, China built a combined power and desalination plant in Zhejiang Province in the 1970s. Since then, salt water has been taken from the East China Sea and converted into fresh water. Some of this fresh water is then sold to industry, some is used in the production of energy, and the remainder is sold as drinking water.

Unfortunately, desalination is an expensive process using large amounts of energy, but research is currently being carried out into the development of more efficient technology using a combination of different methods. To supply water to 25% of the world's population living within 25 kilometres of the sea, more desalination plants are expected to be built in the future. The hope is that the technology currently being developed will lower the costs and help solve the problem of water shortages in many parts of the world.

(380 words)

B Providing water for the world

Global demand for water is increasing as many countries are experiencing large population growth. Even in countries where the water supply is adequate, people are beginning to realize how precious it is. As a result, many countries are developing ways to increase and conserve their supplies of fresh water.

One such solution is desalination, the process by which salt water is converted into drinkable fresh water. This involves the removal of salt compounds and other chemicals from the salt water, a process which has traditionally been carried out by heating the water (the thermal method). The main disadvantage of this method has been the cost. Consequently, a cheaper and more flexible method has been developed, whereby salt water is purified by passing it through membranes. This method is used most effectively in combination with the thermal method.

Since 1958, China, one of the driest countries in the world, has used these two methods to exploit its 32,000-kilometre coastline and convert sea water into fresh water. To maximize efficiency, the Chinese have successfully combined a desalination plant with a power station in Zhejiang Province, using water from the Pacific Ocean to produce fresh water to generate electricity.

In the United Arab Emirates (UAE), desalination has also helped compensate for the lack of natural fresh water. The first desalination plant was established in the UAE in 1960, producing 56,250 litres of fresh water a day. As the demand for fresh water has grown, so has the importance of desalination. Experts forecast that in 2015, 2.7 billion litres of fresh water will be required daily in the UAE, the majority of it being produced by desalination.

The water crisis is not a problem unique to dry countries. In countries with relatively high rainfall, water shortages can still occur because of leakages and the subsequent loss of billions of litres of water. In addition, the average daily consumption of water has risen to as much as 150 litres per person in recent years, due to the increased use of modern technology in our homes. To overcome these problems, the public are encouraged to limit their consumption, and the water companies are being forced to repair pipes.

The demand for water will increase throughout this century, and consequently more countries will turn to desalination as the solution to their decreasing water supplies. However, as water shortages become more widespread due to global warming, this alone will not be enough to solve the problem. Governments will be obliged to ensure that water companies operate efficiently and the public will learn that water is a precious resource to be used economically.

(436 words)

Food chains

7 Look at the diagram of the food chain and answer the questions.

  1 What is a food chain?
    a a type of supermarket
    b a line of people handing out food
    c a group of plants and animals which depend on each other for food

  2 What is usually a producer in a food chain?
    a a plant
    b an animal
    c a person

  3 What is usually a consumer in a food chain?
    a a plant
    b a human or an animal
    c a microrganism

8 Scan the text. Were your answers correct?

9 Check the meanings of the words in the box in a dictionary.

> decomposers   photosynthesis
> herbivores   omnivores   carnivores

10 Read the text more carefully and put the words from exercise 9 in the correct place.

11 **Read Study Skill** Underline six phrases in the text which are used to rephrase or give examples.

STUDY SKILL
Identifying language for rephrasing and giving examples

A well-written text will have discourse markers or signals to help you understand it. They are used for:

- rephrasing or explaining, e.g. *in other words*
- giving examples, e.g. *for instance, for example*

---

12 Read the text more carefully and answer the questions.

  1 What three types of organisms are found in every food chain?
  2 Give an example of each type.
  3 Explain how one organism can be both a primary and a secondary consumer.
  4 What happens to dead animals and plants?

What is a food chain?

A food chain shows the relationship between organisms which feed on each other. This essay will describe the three types of organisms which form food chains, and explain how each organism acts as a food source for the next one in the chain.

The first organism in the food chain cannot feed on other organisms and is called a producer because it makes its own food. Green plants are an example of a producer. They use [1]_____, that is, the process of turning carbon dioxide and water into organic compounds using energy from sunlight. These organic compounds are found in various parts of the plant such as the leaves, fruit, and roots, and are a source of energy for the organism in the next step in the chain, a consumer.

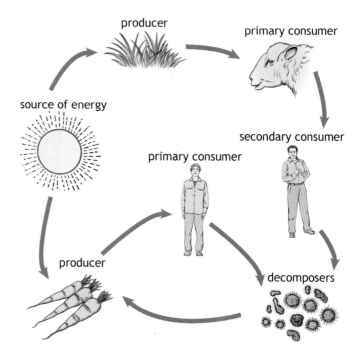

Consumers are generally animals and humans who eat the products of photosynthesis. Examples of this are sheep eating grass, and birds eating seeds. Consumers are classified depending on their place in the chain. For instance, when humans eat vegetables, they are primary consumers. In other words, they are directly eating a product of photosynthesis. When they eat meat, they are secondary consumers. Consumers can also be divided into groups according to what they eat: [2]_____, which eat only plants or plant products, [3]_____, which eat animals, and [4]_____, which eat both plants and animals.

The transfer of energy from one species to another can occur several times, but eventually the chain ends. When the final consumer dies, its body is broken down into simple molecules by [5]_____ such as bacteria and fungi, in the final steps in the chain. These molecules are returned to the soil, where they are used by plants, and the food chain begins again.

To summarize, a food chain shows that every organism is dependent on another for its source of energy, and in turn acts as a food source for the next organism in the chain.

LANGUAGE FOR WRITING Introductions and conclusions

1 Look at the sentences from the essay on page 30. Underline the words and phrases which introduce the topic of the essay or conclude the essay.

   1 This essay will describe the three types of organisms which form food chains, and explain how each organism acts as a food source for the next one in the chain.

   2 To summarize, a food chain shows that every organism is dependent on another for its source of energy, and in turn acts as a food source for the next organism in the chain.

2 Underline the words and phrases which indicate an introduction or conclusion in sentences 1–6.

   1 This report will outline the problems caused by water shortages.

   2 In conclusion, there are two main solutions to this problem.

   3 In brief, it is essential to reduce the pollution of the oceans.

   4 Two aspects of energy conservation will be discussed in this article.

   5 As this report has shown, new developments in technology are essential.

   6 In this paper the problems will be examined in detail and some solutions will be proposed.

3 Add the words and phrases you underlined in exercise 2 to the table.

introductions	summarizing and concluding
This essay will describe …	To summarize, …

Rephrasing and giving examples

4 Look at the extract from the essay on page 30. Underline one phrase which indicates an example and one way of rephrasing.

> Consumers are classified depending on their place in the chain. For instance, when humans eat vegetables, they are primary consumers. In other words, they are directly eating a product of photosynthesis. When they eat meat, they are secondary consumers.

5 Match a word or phrase in A with a way of rephrasing or giving an example in B, and the rest of the sentence in C.

A	B	C
1 Photosynthesis, 2 Primary consumers, 3 A hydro-electric plant, 4 Microorganisms,	in other words, a power station using water to make electricity, for example cows, that is, the process by which plants make food, such as bacteria and fungi,	a will be built on the coast. b feed on plants. c requires sunlight. d are the final step in the food chain.

6 Use a dictionary to complete the sentences.

   1 An important source of energy is carbohydrates, such as _____.

   2 Many people suffer from insomnia, that is, _____.

   3 Respiration, in other words the _____, usually requires oxygen.

   4 Reptiles, for example _____, are cold-blooded, and their bodies are covered in scales.

WRITING Sources of energy

1 **Read Study Skill** Read the title and the introduction to the essay from page 30. Underline the thesis statement.

What is a food chain?

A food chain shows the relationship between organisms which feed on each other. This essay will describe the three types of organisms which form food chains, and explain how each organism acts as a food source for the next one in the chain.

2 Match the thesis statements a–c with the essay titles 1–3.

  a This essay will describe the process of producing petrol from crude oil.

  b This essay examines three renewable sources of energy and outlines the advantages and disadvantages of each one.

  c The consumption of energy has risen considerably due to the growth in the world's population. This has led to the search for new alternative sources of energy.

  1 What are the effects of an increasing population on the world's energy needs?

  2 Describe the process of oil refining.

  3 Discuss renewable sources of energy.

3 Which is the best thesis statement for each essay title?

  1 Discuss the present problems of pollution in the world.

   a Pollution is a serious problem and something should be done about it soon.

   b There are too many cars and these are causing pollution in our cities.

   c There are three major forms of pollution which cities have to deal with.

  `2 Why are plants important?

   a Plants are beautiful and should be respected.

   b Plants are a source of oxygen, food, medicine, and raw materials.

   c Trees are very important because they are needed for the production of wood and paper.

4 **Read Study Skill** Read the essay title *What is solar power?* Using the notes, write a thesis statement and the introduction to the essay.

What is solar power?

- energy from the sun
- uses (heating, cooking, light)
- advantages (cheap to run, doesn't pollute)
- disadvantages (expensive to install, can only be collected in the day time)

The tropical rainforest

5 Read the conclusion from an essay on desalination. Work with a partner. Discuss what information has been included. **Read Study Skill**

> In conclusion, two ways to solve the water crisis have been described: the development of desalination processes and the improved management of water. It is hoped that both can help provide the water which will be needed by a growing population.

STUDY SKILL Conclusions

The conclusion is the final paragraph of an essay. It usually summarizes, evaluates, or discusses consequences.
Do not introduce new information or examples in a conclusion, or repeat words and phrases from the thesis statement.

---

6 Write a concluding paragraph for the essay in exercise 4. Use words and phrases from the *Language for Writing* on page 31 and the notes in the box.

> - solar power – an important source of energy, especially in sunny countries
> - advantages and disadvantages
> - should be further developed

Writing to describe and explain

7 You are going to write an essay (200 words). Choose one of the essay titles, brainstorm some ideas with a partner, and make notes.

- Explain the importance of energy conservation.
- Describe ways to reduce pollution.

8 Select and organize your notes into an introduction, body paragraphs, and a conclusion.

9 Write a thesis statement for your essay.

10 Write the essay, using the *Language for Writing* on page 31.

11 **Read Study Skill** Read through your essay to check the content and organization of each paragraph.

Solar panels

STUDY SKILL Checking your writing (3)

Read your completed essay and ask yourself some questions:
- Does the introduction have a clear thesis statement which outlines the essay?
- Does each paragraph have a topic sentence? (see Study Skill p12)
- Does the conclusion sum up the essay clearly?

Remember to check your essay for accuracy (see Study Skill p9 and p11).

VOCABULARY DEVELOPMENT
Compound nouns and adjectives

1 **Read Study Skill** Underline the compound nouns in each paragraph.

1 There are several tips for succeeding in your studies. Keep good vocabulary records in your notebook. Do your homework regularly. Make sure that your handwriting is easy to read.

2 The Antarctic food chain is a simple example. Plankton, that is, tiny plants that live in sea water, are the producers in this chain. Using carbon dioxide and sunlight, they produce food through photosynthesis and are fed on by krill. Krill are small animals, the primary consumers in this chain. They, in turn, are eaten by whales. The whales are the secondary consumers and the next step in the chain.

3 Music has long been used to treat patients suffering from many different conditions. It has been shown that patients suffering from backache recovered more quickly if they listened to music every morning. A fast heartbeat can also be slowed down by music.

2 Match a noun in 1–6 with a noun a–f to form a compound noun.

1	guide	a	☐	scrapers
2	fossil	b	☐	lines
3	lab	c	☐	case
4	sky	d	☐	fuels
5	mineral	e	☐	coat
6	brief	f	☐	water

3 Complete the sentences with a compound noun from exercise 2.

1 The official rules for the competition are explained in the _____.

2 Anyone carrying out experiments must wear a _____.

3 _____ are characteristic of many modern cities.

4 The government decided to find alternative energy sources and decrease dependency on _____.

5 Water from the spring was purified, bottled, and sold as _____.

6 The missing _____ contained important documents.

4 **Read Study Skill** Complete the sentences in column B with a compound adjective made from the words in italics in column A.

A	B
1 The farm was of a *medium size*.	a It was a **medium-sized** farm.
2 Reservoirs are lakes *made by man*.	b Reservoirs are _____ lakes.
3 The population is *growing fast*.	c The country has a _____ population.
4 The essay was *written well*.	d It was a _____ essay.
5 Make a list of words that *occur frequently*.	e Make a list of _____ words.
6 The produce was all *grown at home*.	f It was all _____ produce.
7 The factory was *built well*.	g It was a _____ factory.
8 A cold does not *threaten* your *life*.	h A cold is not a _____ illness.
9 The costs *increased rapidly* but no one complained.	i No one complained about the _____ costs.
10 Singapore is famous for *building boats*.	j Singapore is famous for its _____ industry.

REVIEW

1 Write a thesis statement for the essay titles 1–3.

   1 What is global warming?
   2 Discuss the importance of reducing pollution.
   3 Explain the dangers of a bad diet.

2 Using the notes, write a conclusion for an essay about the advantages of wind energy.

   - *a free source of energy*
   - *useful in windy countries*
   - *inexpensive to run*
   - *already in use in some countries*

3 Complete the paragraph on respiration, using phrases from the box.

for example   in other words   such as   that is

   Respiration, [1]_____,the process by which living things produce energy from food, usually requires oxygen. Organic compounds [2]_____ glucose are broken down with the oxygen to produce carbon dioxide and water, and energy is released. This energy is necessary for all the functions of the body, [3]_____ growth, movement, and reproduction. Some living things use anaerobic respiration, [4]_____, they do not use oxygen to break down the organic compound.

Wind turbines

4 Are these compound words written as one word, as two words, or are they hyphenated? Look back through Units 1–4 or use a dictionary to help.

   1 note books
   2 well organized
   3 lunch time
   4 English speaking
   5 comprehensive school
   6 fossil fuel
   7 stomach ache
   8 rain water
   9 news paper

5 Complete the sentences with compound adjectives formed from the words in brackets.

   1 Many people suffer from _____ allergies. (related to diet)

   2 Governments are recommending _____ measures to conserve supplies. (save water)

   3 It was a _____ and a successful company. (managed well)

   4 The research scientist encouraged active participation in the _____ process. (make decisions)

   5 Many families in the city have to live in _____ apartment blocks. (maintain poorly)

5 Free trade and fair trade

READING SKILLS Distinguishing between facts, speculation, and reported opinions • Identifying a point of view
LANGUAGE FOR WRITING Expressing certainty, uncertainty, and caution
WRITING SKILLS Supporting a point of view • Presenting arguments (1) and (2) • Writing an opinion essay
VOCABULARY DEVELOPMENT Using a dictionary (3)

READING Globalization

1 Discuss the questions with a partner.

1 What does your country export to other countries?
2 What does it import?
3 What do you understand by the term 'globalization'?

2 Read the title of the text on page 37. What is your opinion?

3 Skim the text. Answer the questions.

1 How many parts are there?
2 How many arguments are there in favour of globalization?
3 How many arguments are there against globalization?
4 What is the writer's opinion on globalization?

4 Scan the text. What are the main arguments *for* and *against* globalization?

5 **Read Study Skill** Find …

1 five expressions expressing caution and generalizations
2 two modal verbs showing uncertainty
3 one adverb showing certainty or uncertainty
4 five reporting verbs showing opinion

6 Read the article. Is the information in sentences 1–7 expressed as a fact (**F**) or speculation (**S**) in the text? How did you decide?

1 International trade is responsible for the increase in world economic growth. **S**
2 The world economy has increased substantially since the 1960s.
3 Average income in China has increased in the last 20 years.
4 Countries which produce coffee import the packaging.
5 Two-way trade results in commercial development in both countries.
6 Farmers are made to sell their products at a low price.
7 Large debts are acquired by countries which import goods.

7 Scan the article again to complete the collocations.

1 international __trade___
2 the global _____
3 world _____
        _____
4 a _____ increase
5 the _____ majority
6 a _____ improvement
7 a _____ benefit
8 manufactured _____
9 an inflated _____
10 a _____ flaw

> **STUDY SKILL**
> **Distinguishing between facts, speculation, and reported opinions**
>
> Facts are statements which are certain or true. Speculation is something which is not necessarily certain or true. To speculate, a writer will use:
>
> - generalizations, e.g. *in general, tend to, have a tendency to*
> - expressions showing caution, e.g. *it would seem/appear*
> - adverbs and adjectives to show varying degrees of certainty, e.g. *probably, possibly, likely, unlikely*
> - modal verbs to show uncertainty, e.g. *may, might*
>
> When a writer wishes to make clear that an opinion is not their own, they use:
>
> - verbs for reporting opinions, e.g. *suggest, believe, argue, claim, maintain*
>
> It is important in your reading to be able to distinguish between facts and opinions.

import

export
globalization

Globalization: is it a force for good or for bad?

Globalization is defined in many ways. One simple definition is that it is the rapid increase in international free trade, investment, and technological exchange. It is argued that this international trade has been one of the main causes of world economic growth over the past half century. Although there is little doubt that the global economy has grown enormously in the last 50 years, some people believe that this growth has only benefitted certain countries, and that others have suffered as a result. Which argument is correct?

Improved income?

An argument in favour of globalization is that the benefits of increased international trade are shared among everyone in the country. An example of this is China, where per capita income rose from about $1400 in 1980 to over $4000 by 2000. Similarly, per capita income rose by over 100% in India between 1980 and 1996. It would appear that countries which open their doors to world trade tend to become wealthier.

However, these sorts of figures might not be giving a true picture. They are 'average' figures, and despite the fact that there has been a substantial increase in income for a small minority of people, the vast majority have only seen a slight improvement.

More imports, more exports

Supporters of free trade point out that there is another direct benefit to be gained from an increase in international trade: exports require imports. Coffee is cited as an example. Countries which produce and export coffee import the packaging for it: a two-way trade which enables commerce to develop in two countries at the same time.

Critics maintain that, in general, it is poorer countries which produce and export food such as coffee, and richer countries which produce and export manufactured goods such as packaging materials. Furthermore, it is the richer countries which control the price of commodities and, therefore, farmers may be forced to sell their produce at a low price and to buy manufactured goods at an inflated price.

Freight terminal in Valparaiso, Chile

Industrial development

Finally, globalization often encourages a country to focus on industries which are already successful. These countries develop expertise and increase their share in the international market. On the other hand, those countries which continue to support all their industries usually do not develop expertise in any one. Consequently, these countries do not find a world market for their goods and do not increase their gross domestic product (GDP) or gross national product (GNP).

Anti-globalists claim that there is a serious flaw in this argument for the specialization of industry. Countries which only focus on one or two main industries are forced to import other goods. These imported goods are frequently over-priced, and these countries, therefore, have a tendency to accumulate huge debts.

This debate will undoubtedly continue for some time. However, it would seem that a better balance between free trade and fair trade is the answer to the problems of globalization.

(495 words)

8 Complete the sentences with a collocation from exercise 7.

1 A reduction in the cost of flying has led to a _____ _____ in international tourism.

2 India and China's share of the _____ _____ is expected to increase over the next ten years.

3 The experiment had to be repeated because there was a _____ _____ in the equation.

4 Holiday packages are often sold at an _____ _____ during peak seasons such as school holidays.

Is 'fair trade' fair?

9 Skim the letters. Which letter is …

1 positive about fair trade?
2 more negative?
3 more objective? **Read Study Skill**

STUDY SKILL Identifying a point of view

A writer may wish to:
- support an argument
- be critical of an argument
- evaluate an argument critically

It is important you can identify the writer's point of view. Look for the number of arguments presented. Are there:
- more *for* or more *against*?
- a balanced number *for* and *against*?

10 Read the letters more carefully. Underline the positive and negative points of fair trade. Add them to the table.

	positive points	negative points
A		high prices for the goods
B		
C		

11 Match the words taken from the three letters to the correct definition.

1 ☐ substantial   a large and important in amount
2 ☐ profit margin   b morally correct
3 ☐ organic   c people selling goods to the public in shops
4 ☐ exploited   d produced without using artificial chemicals
5 ☐ retailers   e the percentage of total sales which is profit
6 ☐ ethical   f used unfairly

A

Sir, with reference to your recent article on fair trade, I would like to point out that although fair trade seems to be a good idea, there are problems. One of these concerns the pricing of fair trade goods. The prices that supermarkets charge for fair trade goods have been analysed. The results show that some retailers are charging extremely high prices for these goods. Moreover, they are not passing on the increase in profits to the producers, which is the purpose of fair trade.

As far I am concerned, fair trade needs to maintain strict control on the pricing policy of goods carrying its label in order to ensure that fair trade remains fair and ethical.

Yours
Ralph Lee

B

Sir, with regard to your article on the fair trade movement, I would like to argue that we are still in the relatively early stages of this movement and it is, therefore, impossible to judge it at present.

I think most people would agree that the fair trade movement is successfully making consumers more aware of how their food is produced. Equally, there is strong evidence that farmers and trades people in poorer countries benefit as a result of their membership of this movement.

However, one could also argue that consumers' desire for fair trade food encourages them to buy foodstuffs that are flown in from abroad. This leads to an increase in air transport, which is bad for the environment. Also, encouraging poorer farmers to produce food for money may lead to a decrease in the production of food for their own country.

It is my opinion that we need to wait a little longer before we truly understand the overall impact of the fair trade movement.

Yours
Jan Montgomerie

C

Sir, with reference to the article 'Is "fair trade" fair?', I wish to say that there can be no question that the fair trade movement has resulted in substantial improvements for small farmers and producers in developing countries.

Fair trade started over 20 years ago to make sure that the profit from the production of food such as coffee or bananas went to the people who produced it, and not to an international company. Previously, many farmers had to sell their produce at a fixed, low price to other people or companies, who then sold it at a great profit.

Today, fair trade also helps producers to organize their own marketing and selling. This way they can demand a higher price and benefit from higher profit margins, which they can then re-invest to improve production. At the same time, high-quality, often organic, food is available to consumers at a reasonable price. They can buy this food knowing that no one was exploited in its production.

In my opinion, this is a win-win situation.

Yours
Philippa Schofield   (467 words)

LANGUAGE FOR WRITING
Expressing certainty and uncertainty

might
could
may
possible **certainly**
likely

1 Underline the modal verbs which show uncertainty.

1 India could be one of the major economic powers of this century.

2 Small companies might also benefit from the increase in world trade.

3 More globalization may have a negative impact on the environment.

2 Rewrite the statements to make them less certain, using the words in brackets.

1 Buying more fair trade food leads to an increase in the use of planes. (may)

2 Globalization has an effect on local culture and traditions. (could)

3 An increase in exports leads to an increase in the number of jobs. (might)

3 Complete the table with adverbs which show degrees of certainty and uncertainty.

4 Complete the sentences with a suitable adjective or adverb to illustrate your point of view. Discuss your answers with a partner.

1 One _____ result of China's greater economic power is that the Chinese language will be taught in schools all over the world. However, it is _____ that this will happen in the near future.

2 An increased demand for fresh water will _____ result in the greater use of desalination plants. It is also _____ that the cost of tap water will go up.

3 It is _____ that the world's population is increasing. An increasing population will _____ lead to an increasing demand for food.

more certain

adjectives	adverbs
certain	certainly
clear	
probable	
likely	
possible	
unlikely	

less certain

Expressing caution

5 Read part of an essay about the effects of globalization on tourism. Underline two verb phrases, one which expresses caution and one which indicates a generalization.

> As globalization increases, the differences between countries disappear. As a result, an increasing number of people are choosing to take holidays in more remote places which are less affected by this. Although there has been a tendency for people to go to 'popular' tourist destinations, it would seem that an increasing number prefer to visit countries where English is not widely spoken, and where they have the opportunity to learn a few words of a new language.

6 Complete the gaps in the next part of the essay with words or phrases from the box.

> believe   could/may   it is likely   it would appear

> ¹_____, however, that the number of people choosing to visit more remote locations is growing too rapidly, and social scientists ²_____ that this increase ³_____ have a negative impact on these locations. They say ⁴_____ that with a rising number of visitors, there will be a rise in the demand for familiar food and in the expectation that local people will speak English. These demands ⁵_____ result in the destruction of the very things which made the destination different from ordinary tourist destinations.

WRITING Examples of fair trade

1 Read the paragraph about fair trade. Which sentence(s) gives …

a the main point?   b the support?   c an example? **Read Study Skill**

> (1) The fair trade movement improves the lives of people in the developing world. (2) In particular, it helps small producers such as farmers and fishermen to plan their futures. (3) One example of this is Antonio, a farmer in South America, who was given a guaranteed price for his coffee for two years. (4) This meant he could calculate his profit margins and, as a result, invest in new equipment for future seasons.

STUDY SKILL Supporting a point of view

When you are presenting a written argument, include:

- the main point(s) in a topic sentence, e.g. *Fair trade should be supported.*
- support, e.g. *It helps small producers in the developing world.*
- a specific example, e.g. *For example, Lami, a fair trade fisherman from Indonesia, now has a small co-operative business with four other fishermen from his village.*

Use expressions such as *for example, an illustration of this is . . . , one example of this is . . .*

---

2 Write a paragraph (100 words) supporting fair trade, using the notes.

> ### Fair trade
> 1 main points
> - Encourages development of the local communities.
> - Helps to reduce environmental damage.
>
> 2 support
> - Many fair trade producers use systems which allow the soil to recover naturally without chemicals.
> - Producers of fair trade goods use their financial and technical expertise in their communities.
>
> 3 examples
> - A coffee co-operative in Mexico started a public bus service in the village.
> - Producers of organic rice in Thailand use traditional techniques which do not use chemicals or exhaust the soil.

Consumerism

3 Work with a partner. Read the essay title.

Is increased consumerism a good thing?

What do you understand by the term *consumerism*?

4 Look at the notes on the possible results of an increase in consumerism in food. Which results are positive and which ones are negative?

a more waste packaging to dispose of
b more choice and variety for customers
c more transport needed (planes)
d more pollution
e more jobs
f more jobs, but in low paid areas, such as farming, packaging, and sales
g more money in local and national economies

5 Work with a partner. Brainstorm and make notes on the possible results of an increase in consumerism in these areas.

- cars • tourism • clothes

Waste packaging

6 [Read Study Skill] Read the beginning of two essays. Will the arguments be presented by topic or by viewpoint in each essay?

> **A** This essay will describe the possible results of an increase in consumerism. It will examine its impact in four main areas, namely food, transport, tourism, and clothing.
>
> **B** This essay will argue that there are clear disadvantages as well as advantages to a rise in consumerism. It will describe the possible adverse effects on the environment and the labour force, and then go on to discuss how the consumer, the producer, and the economy could benefit.

STUDY SKILL
Presenting arguments (1)

In academic writing it is important to present arguments in a consistent way. You can do this:

- by topic, e.g. a paragraph on food (positive and negative), then a paragraph on cars (positive and negative)

or

- by viewpoint, e.g. paragraph(s) on the positive points, then paragraph(s) on the negative points

7 Look at the sentences which start other paragraphs in the two essays in exercise 6. Which sentences belong to essay A and which to essay B?

> 1 Another strong argument is that increased consumption is likely to produce a need for a larger workforce. Unfortunately, this workforce could well be expected to work in poor conditions and for low pay.
>
> 2 The main argument against increased consumerism is that it will almost certainly have a negative effect on the environment.
>
> 3 The second point to be considered is the effect of an increase in the demand for transport.
>
> 4 In the first place, it is clear that an increase in the consumption of foodstuffs will lead to an increase in the amount of packaging needed, for example aluminium tins.

8 Which sentences in exercise 7 introduce the first body paragraph of the essays? Which sentences introduce the second body paragraph? [Read Study Skill]

STUDY SKILL Presenting arguments (2)

It is important to stage your arguments clearly. Use words and phrases such as:
The main argument (for/against ...) is / In the first place, ... / Firstly, ...
Another strong argument is ... / In the second place, ... / Secondly, ...
It is also important to note that ... /Another point is ...
Lastly, ... / Finally, ...

Writing an opinion essay

9 You are going to write the essay on consumerism. Look at the notes from exercises 4 and 5. Decide how to present your arguments (topic or viewpoint). Follow these stages.

- Decide the viewpoint you are writing from. Are you in favour of increased consumerism, against it, or neutral?
- Put your arguments into the order you will present them in an essay.
- Write a thesis statement of one or two sentences for your essay, stating your viewpoint and how you will present your arguments.

10 Write an essay (200–250 words). Use words and phrases from *Language for Writing* on page 39.

in favour

neutral

against

VOCABULARY DEVELOPMENT Multiple meanings

1 Read Study Skill Look at the entry for *fair* from the *Oxford Student's Dictionary*. Write the number of the entry which corresponds to each use of *fair* in the following sentences.

1 Every year there is a huge book *fair* in Beijing and Frankfurt. **2 (2)**
2 He paid us a *fair* price for the goods.
3 Fixing prices is not *fair* to farmers in developing countries.
4 The weather will be *fair* tomorrow.
5 When I was a child, I loved going to the *fair* with my parents.
6 I think we have a *fair* chance of getting the contract.
7 Many Scandinavians have *fair* hair.

2 What part of speech are the underlined words?

1 a In the <u>past</u> people earned less money than they do now.
  b Exports have gone <u>past</u> the billion dollar mark.

2 a The factory workers met to decide whether to have a <u>strike</u> or not.
  b In a storm lightning can <u>strike</u> trees and tall buildings.

3 a Your report must be completely <u>objective</u>.
  b Our <u>objective</u> is to encourage fairer trading.

4 a Wait a <u>second</u>! I'm coming.
  b Our team came <u>second</u> in the competition.

5 a Metals <u>contract</u> as they get cold and expand as they get hot.
  b They will sign the <u>contract</u> tomorrow.

3 Match the underlined words in exercise 2 with a definition. Use your dictionary if necessary.

1 a time before now
  b above or further than a certain point
2 hit
  work stoppage
3 not influenced by your own personal feelings
  aim
4 a short time
  after the first
5 become smaller
  a written legal agreement

4 Complete the sentences, using each word in the box twice.

claimed	lead	ground	movement

1 _____ is a heavy metal.
2 Astronomers chart the _____ of stars and planets.
3 After the heavy rain the _____ was very muddy.
4 The chairman will _____ the discussions.
5 Coffee beans are roasted and then _____ into small particles.
6 The earthquake _____ many lives.
7 The fair trade _____ is growing quickly.
8 The research team _____ to have found a new cure for malaria.

STUDY SKILL Using a dictionary (3)

Words in English can have more than one meaning, pronunciation, or part of speech. For example, they can be a verb and an adjective.

*They **live** near the university.*
*The programme was **live** from the football stadium.*

- Decide what part of speech a word is. This helps you choose the correct entry in a dictionary.
- When you look up a word in the dictionary, look for numbers which show you if there is more than one main entry or more than one meaning.
- Look at the pronunciation. It can change when the word is used in different ways.

fair¹ 🔊 /feə(r)/ *adj., adv.* **1** appropriate and acceptable in a particular situation: *That's a fair price for that house.* ◊ *I think it's fair to say that the number of homeless people is increasing.* **OPP** unfair **2** ~ (to/on sb) treating each person or side equally, according to the law, the rules, etc.: *That's not fair – he got the same number of mistakes as I did and he's got a better mark.* ◊ *It wasn't fair on her to ask her to stay so late.* ◊ *a fair trial* **OPP** unfair **3** quite good, large, etc.: *They have a fair chance of success.* **4** (used about the skin or hair) light in colour: *Chloe has fair hair and blue eyes.* **5** (used about the weather) good, without rain
IDM **fair enough** (*spoken*) used to show that you agree with what sb has suggested
fair play (SPORT) equal treatment of both/all sides according to the rules: *The referee is there to ensure fair play during the match.*
(more than) your fair share of sth (more than) the usual or expected amount of sth

fair² /feə(r)/ *noun* [C] **1** (*also* **funfair**) a type of entertainment in a field or park. At a fair you can ride on machines or try and win prizes at games. Fairs usually travel from town to town. **2** (BUSINESS) a large event where people, businesses, etc. show and sell their goods: *a trade fair* ◊ *the Frankfurt book fair*

fairground /'feəɡraʊnd/ *noun* [C] a large outdoor area where a FAIR is held

fair-'haired *adj.* with light-coloured hair **SYN** blond

REVIEW

1 Read the letter about organic food and answer the questions.

  1 Is the writer positive, negative, or neutral about the production of organic food?

  2 How many arguments are there in favour of organic food?

  3 How many arguments are there against organic food?

> Sir,
>
> In my opinion, your article on organic food was rather one-sided. While I would agree that using fewer chemicals is probably better for the environment, it is not proven scientifically that the food itself is healthier for the consumer than food produced using chemical products.
>
> Furthermore, organic food is much more expensive than ordinary food and, therefore, the majority of people cannot afford to buy it. Unless the price is cut drastically, the overall benefit to the environment is likely to be insignificant as people will continue to buy ordinary food.
>
> Yours
>
> Alan Brown

2 Look at the notes about IT skills. Which ones show:

  1 the main argument?   3 examples?

  2 support for the argument?

> ## IT skills
> 1 good IT (information technology) skills essential
> 2 IT skills demanded by employers
> 3 need IT skills in managerial work, accountancy, retail jobs, etc.
> 4 not always easy for students to find recent books/journals
> 5 students need information for studies

3 Use the notes in exercise 2 to write a paragraph (75–100 words) about IT.

4 Look at the sentences. What part of speech are the words in bold?

  1 In China per capita income **rose** from about $1400 in 1980 to $4000 in 2006.

  2 An increasing number of people are choosing to take holidays in **remote** places.

  3 It was difficult to calculate the profit **margin**.

  4 The prices that supermarkets **charge** for fair trade goods have been analysed.

  5 Which argument is **correct**?

5 Look at the sentences. What part of speech are the missing words?

  1 When you type your essays, please leave a _____ on both sides of the page.

  2 The examiner will _____ your papers and return them next week.

  3 The _____ is the national flower of Iraq, the Maldives, and Romania.

  4 The assistant director took _____ when the director was unwell.

  5 It is not unusual today for families to have several _____ controls, one for the TV, one for the DVD player, and another for their CD player.

6 Complete the sentences in exercise 5 with the words in bold from exercise 4. Use your dictionary to help.

6 Conserving the past

READING SKILLS Dealing with longer texts (1) and (2)
LANGUAGE FOR WRITING Indicating reason or result • Adding information
WRITING SKILLS Checking your writing (4) • Writing an evaluation essay
VOCABULARY DEVELOPMENT Collocations (2)

READING The Terracotta Army

1 Work with a partner. Name three important historic places around the world and two in your country.

2 **Read Study Skill** Survey the text on pages 45 and 46 and answer the questions.

   1 What is the title of the text?
   2 How many parts are there?
   3 What do the photographs show?

STUDY SKILL Dealing with longer texts (1)

To read longer texts effectively, make sure you have enough time for the task and do the following:

Survey
- See Study Skill p4

Question
Ask yourself: What do I already know? What do I want to know? Make questions:
What... ? Where... ? When... ? Why... ?

Read
- First, skim the text (see Study Skill p4). Is the information you need there?
- Secondly, scan the text. Answer as many of your questions as possible.
- Then read the text intensively (see Study Skill p6), and highlight useful information. Underline any key vocabulary.
- Read the highlighted parts of the text again and make notes to answer your questions.

---

3 Look at the pairs of words. Which word in each pair would you expect to find in the text *Ancient China's Terracotta Army*?

   1 Emperor/President   4 Brazilian/Chinese
   2 archer/pilot   5 chariot/helicopter
   3 plastic/terracotta

4 Make questions from the prompts.

   1 When/find?   **When was the army found?**
   2 Where/ find?
   3 When/ build?
   4 Who/ build?
   5 How many/ find?
   6 How many/visit?

5 Skim the text to locate which paragraphs will contain the answers to your questions in exercise 4. Write the paragraph letter next to your question.

6 Scan the text to answer your questions in exercise 4.

Ancient China's Terracotta Army

A One of the greatest archaeological finds of all time is the Terracotta Army of ancient China. Discovered accidentally in 1974, in Qin province, in China, when local farmers were digging for water, over 8,000 baked clay, or terracotta, figures have since been found (fig. 1).

Qin's army

B It is now known that Emperor Qin Shi Huang ordered this clay army to be built at the beginning of the third century BCE. Emperor Qin was one of the most important rulers in Chinese history. After becoming emperor of the state of Qin at the age of 13, he conquered six other states over the next 25 years, and became the first emperor of a united China. One of his greatest achievements was the building of the first Great Wall of China to protect China from its enemies. Not all of his achievements were military, however, as he also introduced a common form of writing throughout the country. Nevertheless, outside China he is most famous for his terracotta army.

C In Qin's time, the ancient Chinese believed that their 'afterlife' was very similar to their life on earth. Consequently, when they died and were buried, objects which would be useful to them in the next life were buried with them. Emperor Qin was no different; he started the building of his own mausoleum, or burial place, in about 246 BCE. More than 700,000 workers and craftsmen took 38 years to complete the huge imperial palace, offices, and halls, all surrounded by a wall. In addition, the emperor ordered an army to be built so that his palace would be protected.

Building an army

D Elsewhere in the ancient world, craftsmen concentrated on one piece of work at a time. In ancient China, however, they used a completely different method. A huge production line was established to make the tens of thousands of individual human and animal statues which Emperor Qin demanded. All the different parts of the body such as legs, arms, and heads were made separately and then assembled. The same process was also used for other pieces such as ears, beards, and armour. When the whole figure was completed, it was baked in a kiln, or oven.

E The terracotta figures are life-like and life-sized. Each one has a different facial expression and hairstyle, as well as uniforms which indicate their job and rank. Amongst the figures there are ordinary soldiers (fig. 2), archers, and officers, together with chariots and horses (fig. 3). They were discovered arranged in military formation ready to protect the emperor in the afterlife.

Figure 1

Figure 2

Figure 3

Destruction and preservation

F Excavations have shown that there was a serious fire, which is thought to have lasted for three months, shortly after Emperor Qin's death. It is believed that an invading army robbed the emperor's tomb and then set fire to it. The roofs of the buildings collapsed and fell onto the soldiers and horses. As a result, not one of the statues remained complete or undamaged. Many, in fact, were damaged extensively and some were destroyed completely.

G Repairing and preserving these figures has become the highest priority (fig. 4). Skilled workers search methodically through hundreds of thousands of fragments to find the right piece to complete each figure. They are lucky if they find one matching piece a day. Because of this, each statue takes several months to be repaired. Furthermore, when the first statues were exposed to the air for the first time in over two thousand years, the paint on them started peeling off or turning black. After extensive research to try and find ways to prevent this problem, scientists now use a chemical solution to protect the paintwork.

Figure 4

The Terracotta Army today

H In 1987, the tomb and army of Emperor Qin were declared a World Heritage site by UNESCO (the United Nations Educational, Scientific, and Cultural Organization). Only places which have outstanding importance to all people around the world are given this title. The Terracotta Army clearly deserves this honour, as nearly two million people from all over the world visit it each year (fig. 5).

(680 words)

Figure 5

7 Read the text intensively. Highlight the information on topics 1–5.

1 Emperor Qin's achievements
2 ancient Chinese beliefs about the 'afterlife'
3 the way the ancient Chinese craftsmen worked
4 how the statues got damaged
5 preserving the statues

8 Make notes about the topics in exercise 7, using the information you highlighted.

9 Cover the text. Use your notes and what you recall from the text to answer the questions.

1 What were Emperor Qin's major achievements?
2 Why did the ancient Chinese bury things with the dead?
3 How did Chinese craftsmen work differently from craftsmen of other ancient countries?
4 What were the main causes of the damage to the statues?
5 How are the statues being preserved?

10 Compare your answers with the original information in the text. What information, if any, did you leave out or note incorrectly?

Read Study Skill

11 Choose ten new words or phrases from the text which you could use in your academic studies. Compare your choices with a partner and explain some of your words to your partner. Record your words appropriately.

LANGUAGE FOR WRITING Indicating reason or result

1 Look at the underlined words in the sentences from the text. Do they indicate *reason* or *result*?

   1 In Qin's time, the ancient Chinese believed that their 'afterlife' was very similar to their life on earth. <u>Consequently</u>, when they died and were buried, objects which would be useful to them in the next life were buried with them.
   2 In addition, the emperor ordered an army to be built <u>so that</u> his palace would be protected.
   3 The roofs of the buildings collapsed and fell onto the soldiers and horses. <u>As a result</u>, not one of the statues remained complete or undamaged.

2 Add the underlined words and phrases to the table. Make a note of the punctuation.

3 Find more words and phrases which show *reason* or *result* in the sentences. Add them to the table.

showing reason	showing result

   1 Venice is sinking because of the rising level of the sea.
   2 Archaeologists study ancient objects in order to learn about ancient cultures.
   3 The fire in the museum resulted in extensive damage.
   4 Visitors to the art exhibition are not permitted to use flash photography since this can cause damage to the pictures.
   5 Historic monuments are expensive to maintain, so it is often necessary to charge an entry fee.
   6 A new museum is being built as the collections are too large for the present museum.
   7 The construction of the Aswan dam and lake would have destroyed the ancient temple of Abu Simbel. Therefore, it was decided to move the temple to a new site.

RULES Reason or result

Look at the words and phrases used to show *reason* or *result*, and the structures which follow them.

so, **so that**, **because**, **since**, **as** + subject + verb

because of + noun clause

in order to + infinitive

As a result, **Consequently**, and **Therefore** are often used at the beginning of a second sentence.

---

4 Read the rules. Match the beginnings and ends of the sentences. Then join the two parts, using a word or phrase showing *reason* or *result*.

	because		
1 Large numbers of people from all over the world visit Petra, in Jordan,	because of	a	it is important for them to learn about the history of their country.
2 Children are encouraged to visit museums	so	b	the ancient buildings are hidden below modern buildings.
3 Historians are often required to learn languages such as Latin	As a result,	c	its beauty.
4 Some cities, like Rome, have been inhabited for thousands of years	in order to	d	the city was particularly well preserved.
5 In 79 CE Pompeii was covered by a thick layer of volcanic ash from Mount Vesuvius.		e	read ancient manuscripts and inscriptions.

Adding information

5 Look at the sentences from the text on page 45. Underline the words which add information.

  1 One of his greatest achievements was the building of the first Great Wall of China to protect China from its enemies. Not all of his achievements were military, however, as he also introduced a common form of writing throughout the country.

  2 More than 700,000 workers and craftsmen took 38 years to complete the huge imperial palace, offices, and halls, all surrounded by a wall. In addition, the emperor ordered an army to be built so that his palace would be protected.

6 Find and underline other words which add information. Make a note of the punctuation.

  1 Museums are important centres for research. Moreover, many have laboratories for preserving ancient objects.

  2 Petra is of major historic significance as well as being a place of great beauty.

  3 Studying history helps us to understand the past. Furthermore, it can help our understanding of the present.

  4 Archaeological excavations often take a long time to complete. What is more, they can be very expensive.

7 Link the pairs of sentences twice, using the words and phrases of addition in brackets.

  1 Museums need extensive funding for research. Money is required to exhibit the objects properly and safely. (Furthermore/Moreover)

  2 Machu Picchu is Peru's most important ancient monument. It is one of the new seven wonders of the world. (also/as well as)

  3 The Hermitage Museum in St. Petersburg has over three million objects which visitors can admire. The collection can be seen on the museum's website. (What is more/In addition)

WRITING Museums

1 **Read Study Skill** Read paragraph A only of the essay on page 49. Answer the questions.

  1 What is the purpose of the essay?

  2 Is the purpose clearly expressed?

2 Read the notes for an essay on the role of museums. Compare them with paragraphs B and C. Answer the questions about the notes.

  1 Are all the main points included?

  2 Are there examples for the main points?

  3 Has any irrelevant information been included?

---

1 Education

1.1 *clear exhibition of objects*

1.2 *clear explanation of objects*

1.3 *educate people in a country*

1.4 *educate people from other countries + example*

2 Research

2.1 *exhibitions only good if information correct – must do research*

2.2 *need to know how 1 object connects to others – how object developed + example*

STUDY SKILL
Checking your writing (4)

After completing the first draft of your essay, put it aside for a while. It is easier to check the content with 'fresh' eyes. Check for:

Purpose

Is the purpose of the essay to *describe*, *explain*, *persuade*, *analyse*, *discuss*, *compare*, or *evaluate*?

Content

Does the essay:
- introduce the topic clearly?
- include all the main points?
- exclude irrelevant or inappropriate information?
- give examples and explanations?
- conclude appropriately?

Organization
- Are the ideas in a logical order?
- Is the writing divided into paragraphs?
- Are ideas linked appropriately?

The role of museums

A This essay will describe and evaluate the purpose of museums, namely to educate, research, and conserve. Furthermore, it will argue that museums are an essential part of any society or culture.

B The primary function of any museum is to educate the general public by exhibiting historical objects which have been found. Museums provide clear descriptions of these objects. They explain where they are from, when they were made, how they were made, and what they were used for. Museums help us to understand our history. What is more, people can learn about the history and culture of other countries. The exhibition of Tutankhamen's tomb is a good example of this. The number of gold objects found in the tomb was extremely impressive. This exhibition travelled the world and taught people about ancient Egypt.

C However, exhibitions are only useful if objects are correctly described and explained. There should be a text describing each object and its origins. In order to do this, historians and archaeologists in the museum have to do extensive research. Unless it is understood how an object relates to other objects from the same period, and from earlier and later periods, it is not possible to understand the development of that object. For example, ancient glass bottles have been found all over the world. It was only through research, however, that archaeologists realized that glass blowing probably started sometime towards the end of the first century BCE. Syrian craftsmen were probably the first to use this new technology, which subsequently spread throughout Europe, and eventually to China.

The Louvre, Paris

The Egyptian Museum, Cairo

3 Cross out one irrelevant sentence in paragraphs B and C.

Writing an evaluation essay

4 Read the essay title.

The role of historic sites.

Write the introduction to the essay. Remember to include a thesis statement explaining the purpose of your essay, and giving your opinion.

5 Look at the notes for the next two paragraphs for the essay. Cross out one piece of irrelevant information from each list.

1 Education

1.1 show clearly how people used to live/work

1.2 easier for children to learn and understand than books, etc. + example

1.3 can learn from earlier technologies

1.4 fun day out for the family

2 Tourism

2.1 many visitors want to visit historic sites + example

2.2 visitors bring money into local + national economy

2.3 visitors take many photographs to show their friends

2.4 visitors understand more about our culture and history

6 Write the two paragraphs, using the notes in exercise 5. Give examples. Use words and phrases from *Language for Writing* on page 47.

7 Write a conclusion to the essay. Summarize the main points and give your opinion.

8 Check your essay for purpose, content, and organization (see Study Skill p48).

VOCABULARY DEVELOPMENT Collocations (2)

1 **Read Study Skill** Read the sentences from the text on page 46. Identify three verb + adverb collocations.

> As a result, not one of the statues remained complete or undamaged. Many, in fact, were damaged extensively and some were destroyed completely.
>
> Skilled workers search methodically through hundreds of thousands of fragments to find the right piece to complete each figure.

STUDY SKILL Collocations (2)

Collocations (see Study Skill p26) can also be formed by:

- verb + adverb, e.g. *damage extensively*
- adverb + adjective, e.g. *completely different*

2 Underline verb + adverb collocations in the sentences.

1 The students listened attentively to Dr Potter's lecture on the excavations at Leptis Magna.
2 Our knowledge of how ancient people lived has improved enormously with the use of new technology such as Global Positioning Systems (GPS).
3 The fire in the museum spread rapidly and caused extensive damage.
4 This essay will concentrate mainly on the events of August 1705.
5 The scientific methods used in archaeology today contrast sharply with the methods used in the 19th century.

3 Underline the adverb or adverbial phrase which collates with the verb. Use a dictionary to help you.

1 The committee felt *strongly/powerfully* that visitors should not be charged an entrance fee to the museum.
2 If I remember *perfectly/correctly*, it was the Nabataeans who built Petra.
3 The city of Leptis Magna expanded *significantly/importantly* in the second century CE.
4 Many ancient objects are discovered *by luck/by chance*.
5 The economy can benefit *largely/enormously* from the revenue produced by visitors to historic sites and museums.
6 It is impossible to describe *precisely/truly* how an ancient people lived, but archaeologists endeavour to give as accurate a picture as possible.

4 Underline two adverb + adjective collocations in the paragraph below.

> Excavations are often carried out by highly-qualified teams of archaeologists helped by local volunteers or workers. Although the work is often painstakingly slow, it can produce fascinating results.

5 Complete the sentences with an adverb + adjective collocation from the box.

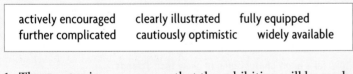

> actively encouraged   clearly illustrated   fully equipped
> further complicated   cautiously optimistic   widely available

1 The curator is _____ that the exhibition will be ready on time.
2 The museum guide book is _____ with photographs and drawings.
3 Most modern museums have _____ research laboratories.
4 These days school children are _____ to visit museums, which put on special displays to educate and inform them.
5 The professor's new book is _____ in school and university libraries.
6 The controversial research was _____ by the resignation of the chief scientist.

REVIEW

1 Read about Sabratha. Add sentences a–d to the text in the correct place.

   a   As a result, many buildings were destroyed and the city had to be rebuilt.
   b   This was because they had been built of very soft sandstone.
   c   What is more, it became an important regional centre.
   d   These include magnificent mosaics and statues.

Sabratha

The majestic ruins of the ancient city of Sabratha lie about 80km west of Tripoli, the capital of Libya. They are the high point of any visit to that country.

It is thought that the original settlement started in the 4th century BCE. However, by the second century BCE, Sabratha was a thriving city. Its success was based on trade north across the Mediterranean and south into Africa for animals and ivory.

In the first century CE, there was a violent earthquake. In the 200 years which followed, the city expanded steadily and became increasingly wealthy. However, when it suffered another earthquake in 365 CE, the buildings simply collapsed.

This time the city never really recovered. It was occupied by various armies until it was abandoned in the 8th century CE. It was rediscovered in the early 20th century CE by archaeologists. Since then, some of the major buildings such as the theatre have been reconstructed and many pieces of artwork have been discovered. These can be seen in the nearby museum.

2 Read the text again. Underline collocations and add them to the table.

adjective + noun	adverb + adjective	verb + adverb
majestic ruins		

3 Look at the notes and the first part of an essay about Machu Picchu. Answer the questions.

   1   What is the purpose of the essay?
   2   Are all the points from the notes included?
   3   Has any irrelevant information been added?
   4   Are the points in a logical order?

> **Machu Picchu**
> 1 Introduction
> 2 Basic information – where and when
> 3 Use
>   3.1 military / commercial /administrative – unlikely
>   3.2 religious / cultural – possible?
> 4 Buildings
>   4.1 types of building
>   4.2 how they were built– technology

4 Read the essay again and correct it.

   1   Put the sentence into the correct place.

      It is, therefore, more likely that it had some religious or cultural function.

   2   Cross out one sentence containing irrelevant information.
   3   Find one sentence in the wrong position and put it in the correct position.

Machu Picchu

This essay will give a brief description of the Inca city of Machu Picchu, in modern day Peru. It will argue that this ancient city is one of the most important archaeological sites in South America.

Machu Picchu is a city located high up in the Andes mountains in Peru. It is an incredibly beautiful location. It was built between 1460 and 1470 CE by an Inca ruler.

It is unlikely that it had any military or commercial functions because it was built so high up and in a fairly inaccessible place. What is more, there is no archaeological or written evidence that it was an administrative centre.

It is clear that they were planned and constructed with great care and precision. There are about 200 buildings at Machu Picchu, including houses, storage structures, temples, and other public buildings. The buildings are made of an extremely hard stone, yet they fit on top of one another perfectly. In fact, they fit so perfectly that it is impossible to put a thin knife blade between the stones. This feat of construction has led archaeologists to speculate about the type of tools which could have been used to cut the stone so perfectly.

READING SKILLS How to make reading easier (1), (2), and (3)
VOCABULARY DEVELOPMENT Suffixes
RESEARCH Avoiding plagiarism (2)
LANGUAGE FOR WRITING Verbs for reporting another writer's ideas
WRITING Summarizing • Writing a summary

READING Feats of engineering

1 Discuss the questions with a partner.
  1 What remarkable man-made structures are there in your country?
  2 What about in other countries?

2 Skim the web page. What three kinds of structure is the text about?

3 Scan the web page and answer the questions.
  1 Where were the tallest buildings in the world in 1999?
  2 How tall are they?
  3 When was the Millau Bridge opened?
  4 How long is the guarantee for the Millau Bridge?
  5 What is the name of the river that the Itaipu Dam crosses?
  6 How much material was removed to build the dam?

---

www.wondersoftheworld.com

Giant structures

*It is an impossible task to select the most amazing wonders of the modern world, since every year more wonderful constructions appear. As soon as the tallest building in the world is completed, another even taller one breaks the record. Even though these constructions are spectacular, the **innovative** technology which they incorporate will undoubtedly be improved on in the future.*

The Petronas Towers

The Petronas Towers were the tallest buildings in the world when they were **inaugurated** in 1999. With a height of 452 metres, the **slender** twin towers, like two thin pencils, dominate the city of Kuala Lumpur. At the 41st floor, the towers are linked by a bridge, symbolizing a gateway to the city. The American architect Cesar Pelli designed the skyscrapers with eight-point star shapes with an Islamic influence to reflect the Muslim culture of Malaysia.

Constructed of high-strength concrete, the building provides around 1,800 square metres of office space on every floor, and includes a shopping centre and a concert hall at the base. Other features of this impressive monument include double-decker lifts, and glass and steel sunshades.

The Millau Bridge

The Millau Bridge was opened in 2004 in the Tarn Valley, in southern France. At the time it was built it was the world's highest bridge, reaching over 340m at the highest point. Described as one of the most **breathtakingly** beautiful bridges in the world, it was built to relieve Millau's congestion problems caused by traffic passing from Paris en route to Barcelona, in Spain.

The bridge is supported by seven concrete and steel pillars which rise into seven graceful pylons. Designed by the British architect Norman Foster and constructed by a French company, it was built to **withstand** the most extreme seismic and meteorological conditions and is guaranteed for 120 years!

The Itaipu Dam

The Itaipu hydroelectric power plant is the largest construction of its kind in the world. It consists of a series of dams across the River Parana, which forms a natural border between Brazil and Paraguay. Started in 1975 and taking 16 years to complete, the construction was carried out as a **joint** project between the two countries.

The dam is remarkable for both its electricity output and its size. In 1995 it produced 78% of Paraguay's and 25% of Brazil's energy needs, breaking previous records for energy production. In its construction, the amount of iron and steel used was equivalent to over 300 Eiffel Towers, and the volume of concrete needed was equal to 210 football stadiums! Furthermore, the **course** of the seventh biggest river in the world was changed and 50 million tons of earth and rock were removed. It is a truly remarkable feat of engineering.

(446 words)

4 Read the web page intensively and answer the questions.

1 What facilities do the Petronas Towers have?
2 What did the architect of the towers want the buildings to reflect?
3 Why was the Millau Bridge built?
4 What is the bridge like?
5 What do you learn about the power produced by the Itaipu Dam?
6 What was special about the construction of the dam?

5 Read Study Skill Complete the table. Guess the meaning of the words in bold in the text. Use the part of speech to help you.

word	part of speech	your guess
innovative	adjective	introducing new ideas

6 Read Study Skill Underline the main clause in the sentences.

> **STUDY SKILL** How to make reading easier (2)
>
> Complex sentences have more than one clause. To help you understand them, identify the main clause.
>
> *Started in 1975 and taking 16 years to complete,* **the construction was carried out as a joint project between the two countries**.
>
> Identify the other clauses by looking for relative pronouns, linking words, and phrases beginning with a present or past participle.
>
> ***Started in 1975 and taking 16 years to complete***, *the construction was carried out as a joint project between the two countries.*

1 It is an impossible task to select the most amazing wonders of the modern world, since every year more wonderful constructions appear.

2 The Petronas Towers were the tallest buildings in the world when they were inaugurated in 1999.

3 Constructed of high-strength concrete, the building provides around 1,800 square metres of office space on every floor, and includes a shopping centre and a concert hall at the base.

4 Described as one of the most breathtakingly beautiful bridges in the world, it was built to relieve Millau's congestion problems caused by traffic passing from Paris en route to Barcelona, in Spain.

5 The bridge is supported by seven concrete and steel pillars which rise into seven graceful pylons.

6 In 1995 it produced 78% of Paraguay's and 25% of Brazil's energy needs, breaking previous records for energy production.

7 Circle the relative pronoun, linking word, or participle, and underline the clauses which they introduce.

1 It is an impossible task to select the most amazing wonders of the modern world, since every year more wonderful constructions appear.

2 The bridge is supported by seven concrete and steel pillars which rise into seven graceful pylons.

3 Designed by the British architect Norman Foster and constructed by a French company, it was built to withstand the most extreme seismic and meteorological conditions and is guaranteed for 120 years!

Islands in the sun

8 Discuss the questions with a partner.

1 What structures can be built in the sea?
2 Why do people want to build in the sea?

9 Skim the web page *The most wonderful islands*, look at the pictures, and answer the questions.

1 What do the pictures show?
2 What is the text about?
3 Where are the Palm Islands?

10 Scan the text and decide if the statements are true (**T**), false (**F**), or not-stated in the text (**NS**).

1 Dutch engineers are sometimes experienced in reclaiming land from the sea.
2 The islands are being built in the deep water of the sea.
3 Rocks to build the breakwater were taken from the desert.
4 All the luxury homes have been sold on Palm Jumeirah.
5 Some famous people have already bought the luxury homes.
6 The Palm Deira will be the same size as Paris.

11 **Read Study Skill** What do the pronouns refer to? Look at the text again. Complete the table.

STUDY SKILL How to make reading easier (3)

Pronouns, e.g. *it*, *this* are used to avoid repetition in a text. Identifying these referents helps you understand a text.

- Backward referencing refers to something which has been mentioned previously, perhaps in another sentence. For example:
  *The sea was very deep with strong tidal movements. **This** made it difficult to build the bridge.*
  *The sand is taken from the desert. **It** is transported by road.*

- Forward referencing refers to something which comes later in the sentence. For example:
  ***It** is surprising that the current and tidal movements are so strong in such shallow water.*

---

pronoun		refers to
They	(line 3)	_____
This	(line 16)	_____
It	(line 22)	_____
it	(line 30)	_____
These	(line 33)	_____

---

www.wondersoftheworld.com

The most wonderful islands

The Palm Islands are the largest artificial islands in the world and are under construction in Dubai, in the United Arab Emirates (UAE). They are being developed as tourist, leisure, and residential resorts, and will increase the coastline of the country by 120 kilometres. 5

After four years of planning and careful consideration of the environmental issues, construction started in 2001. Dutch engineers with experience of reclaiming land from the sea were employed in the building of the first two islands.

The site for all three islands is an area of the sea where the 10 water is not very deep. Sand is taken from the seabed and sprayed into the construction site. Although the shallow water facilitates this process, the islands are still very exposed to the currents and tidal movements of the sea. Rocks are used to hold the sand in place resulting in a 15 large crescent structure. This acts as a breakwater and protects the islands from the sea.

The first two islands are in the shape of date palm trees and consist of a trunk and 17 fronds, or leaves, coming off the trunk. The first island, named Palm Jumeirah, has three 20 five-star hotels in the trunk, and luxury homes in the leaves. It is astonishing that when these homes went on sale in 2004, they were all sold within three days.

The second palm, Jebel Ali, was started in 2002 and is designed to be an entertainment centre. Six marinas are 25 planned, with a water theme park, and homes built on stilts in the water.

The Palm Deira is planned to be the largest of the three islands, with a length of 14 km and a width of 8.5 km, an area larger than the city of Paris. Engineers estimate that it will 30 require a billion cubic metres of rock and sand. It will consist of residential properties, marinas, shopping malls, sports facilities, and clubs. These will be open to both residents and tourists.

More artificial islands, the World Islands, are now being 35 constructed near the Palm Jumeirah. They consist of 300 private islands grouped into the shape of the continents of the world and will be used for estates, private homes, community islands, and resorts.

Unquestionably, these artificial islands are one of the 40 wonders of the modern world. They will also maintain Dubai's status as one of the leading tourist destinations in the region.

(396 words)

VOCABULARY DEVELOPMENT Word-building (1)

1 **Read Study Skill** Look at the words in the box opposite. Underline the suffixes. Use these suffixes to identify the part of speech.

2 Complete the table with different parts of speech. Mark the stressed syllable. Use the Study Skill box on suffixes and a dictionary to help.

verb	noun	adjective	adverb
anályse	análysis / ánalyst	analýtical	analýtically
		(in)consístent	
		(in)decísive	
ecónomize			
			invéntively
	invólvement		
prodúce			
		(in)signíficant	
théorize			

addition	impressive
archaeologist	innovative
artificial	remarkable
breathtakingly	residential
conclusion	seismic
efficiently	successfully
expensively	unnecessarily
experiment	

STUDY SKILL Suffixes

A suffix is a letter or a group of letters which you add at the end of a word. Suffixes change the part of speech and the meaning of the word.

Common endings include:

nouns	-tion, -ance, -ness, -ment
adjectives	-ant, -ive, -able, -ic, -al, -ent
adverbs	-ly, -ily
people	-ist, -yst, -or, -er

---

3 Complete the sentences with the correct form of the word in brackets.

1 The blood sample was sent to the laboratory for _____. (analyse)

2 The student's work has improved _____. (consist)

3 The _____ (decide) was taken early this morning.

4 The students are studying _____. (economize)

5 The company wants to _____ (involve) as many people as possible in the discussions.

6 The discussions were very _____. (produce)

7 The Italian engineer Guglielmo Marchese Marconi was the _____ (invent) of the radio.

8 Costs have risen _____. (signify)

9 Experiments will be carried out to test the _____. (theorize)

4 Complete the paragraph with the correct form of the word in brackets.

The longest road tunnel in the world

The world's longest road tunnel, which was [1]_____ (inauguration) in November 2000, goes from Laerdal to Aurland in Norway and is 24.5 km long. Before the tunnel was built, all traffic had to cross the high mountain passes, which were often closed in the winter because of snow. This tunnel allows the traffic to flow at all times of the year. The tunnel is famous for its state-of-the-art technology. [2]_____ (innovative) ventilation systems have been [3]_____ (installation) to make sure that clean, fresh air is maintained throughout the [4]_____ (long) of the tunnel. In addition, it has [5]_____ (exception) sophisticated safety measures. This [6]_____ (impress) tunnel attracts thousands of tourists each year and has even been used for a wedding.

RESEARCH Crediting sources (1)

Read Study Skill Write out 1–3 as entries in a list of references. Use the APA style shown in the study skill box.

STUDY SKILL Avoiding plagiarism (2)

Writing an essay often involves using information from books, articles, or websites. It is important to acknowledge these sources in a list of references (or bibliography) at the end of your essay.

There are various styles and conventions. Check your department's preferred style and use it consistently. Do not mix styles.

- **Books**: Author surname, Initials. (Date of publication). *Book title*. Place of publication: Publisher.
  Wookey, C. K. (2003). *Modern Buildings*. New York: Harper.
- **Journal articles**: Author surname, Initials. (Date of publication). Article title. *Journal title*, *Volume number*, page numbers.
  Carter, K. A. (1999). Developing technology in developing countries. *Journal of International Sport*, *6*, 132–143.
- **Websites**: Author, if available. *Web page title*. (Date of publication, if available). Date of retrieval, web address
  The wonder club. Retrieved March 15, 2006, from
  http://wonderclub.com/WorldWonders/ModernWonders.html   APA style

1 Book
Title: Building in Challenging Environments
Author: André Matache
Publisher: Wexford University Press
Date of publication: 2005

2 Journal article
Article title: The cost of construction
Author: John Sinden
Name of the journal: The Journal of General Structural Engineering
Volume and page numbers: Volume 4 pp 34–56.
Date of publication: 2004

3 Website
Article title: Artificial Islands
Author: James Smallridge
Web address:
http://www./ulid.man.ac.uk/islandmanagement/
Date you saw this on the Internet (i.e. 'retrieval'):
4 September 2006

LANGUAGE FOR WRITING
Verbs for reporting another writer's ideas

1 Read the summary below of the text *Giant structures*. Underline three verbs which report the ideas of the original writer.

In this article from the website wondersoftheworld.com, the writer presents three different structures that, he argues, should be considered as wonders of the modern world. These three structures have been built in different parts of the world for very different purposes, but all three are amazing for their innovative design, beauty, and size. The author first describes the Petronas Towers in Malaysia. These twin towers were the highest in the world when they were built, dominating the city of Kuala Lumpur. The second construction chosen is the Millau Bridge in France. The writer explains that this bridge was built to reduce the traffic problems in the city, but, because of its beauty, it has become a tourist attraction itself. The third construction is the Itaipu Dam in Paraguay. This huge dam was built on the river between Paraguay and Brazil, and is used to provide water for an enormous hydroelectric power plant.

2 Read the rules. Read the summary below of the text *The most wonderful islands*. Complete the summary with a suitable reporting verb from the box in its correct form.

| describe | explain | argue | believe | claim |

The most wonderful islands is an article which [1]_____ the artificial islands in the UAE. Taken from the website 'wondersoftheworld.com', it [2]_____ that the Palm Islands are one of the wonders of the modern world. The writer [3]_____ how these islands were constructed and why they were built. There are three islands being constructed in the sea from sand and rocks. Each one will have tourist attractions as well as luxury accommodation. The author [4]_____ that these islands are great feats of modern engineering.

RULES Reporting verbs

Use reporting verbs, e.g. *explain*, *describe* when you summarize the ideas of the writer of a text.

These verbs are used in different ways. For example: verb + that + clause, e.g. *explain*, *argue*, *believe*, *claim*:
The writer explains that this bridge was built to reduce the traffic problems in the city.
Verb + noun or indirect question, e.g. *present*, *describe*, *explain*:
The author first describes the Petronas Towers in Malaysia.
The writer explains why the dam was constructed.

WRITING Tunnels and buildings

1 Which simple sentence, a or b, summarizes the sentences and paragraphs 1–3?

1 One serious problem of long tunnels is the somniferous effect. That is to say that the lighting systems and general nature of the tunnels encourage a feeling of sleepiness, and drivers can fall asleep at the wheel.
  a The lighting systems in tunnels can cause problems.
  b Long tunnels can make drivers go to sleep.

2 The tallest buildings in the world, that is, the tallest buildings at the time of writing, are the Petronas Towers, which dominate the skyline of Kuala Lumpur.
  a The Petronas Towers are the highest buildings in the world at the moment.
  b The Petronas Towers dominate the skyline of Kuala Lumpur.

3 Man has built on the land, under the land, on the sea, and under the sea, so perhaps the next choice for construction will be in space. This would offer the possibility of exploiting limitless areas.
  a Man has built in many different areas.
  b Man may build in space.

2 **Read Study Skill** Underline the main ideas in the paragraphs A–C. Compare your answers with a partner.

Shanghai

STUDY SKILL Summarizing

You may be required to write a summary of a text.
- First, identify the main ideas in the paragraph or text.
- Then organize these ideas into a logical order.
- Finally, rewrite these ideas in simple sentences, using linking words.

Remember to use your own words (see Study Skill p14).

A Many countries in the world have a growing population, and in some countries the population is increasing by as much as two per cent every decade. This population expansion results in an increase in the demand for housing, and causes overcrowding.

B One of the most noticeable phenomena in many of today's large capital cities is their increasingly efficient public transport systems. These encourage people to leave their privately-owned vehicles at home.

C High-rise buildings are now common in our big cities. These skyscrapers are seen as a solution to the shortage of available land because, by building vertically rather than horizontally, more accommodation can be obtained from the same surface area.

3 Summarize each of the paragraphs in exercise 2 in one simple sentence.

4 Read the paragraph and underline the five main ideas. Use the prompts 1–5 to help you.

1 What and why? 3 Length? 5 Use?
2 Significance? 4 Date opened?

The longest railway tunnel in the world

Due to an increase in traffic between the various islands which make up Japan, and predictions of a continuing growth in train travel, a rail tunnel was built to connect the islands of Honshu and Hokkaido. The Seikan Tunnel in Japan is today the longest railway tunnel in the world, with a length of almost 54 km. When the tunnel was opened in 1988, all the existing trains between Honshu and Hokkaido went through it. However, newer Japanese bullet trains have never used the tunnel because of the cost of extending the high-speed line through it. Consequently, the train journey from Tokyo to Sapporo still takes about ten hours. In contrast, the journey by air takes only three and a half hours. This, combined with a fall in the cost of flying, has meant that more people travel by plane than train, and the tunnel is not used as much as forecasters had predicted.

5 Organize the ideas you underlined in exercise 4 and write them in two or three sentences using linking words.

6 Read the text about the Sydney Opera House. Use the prompts to identify four main ideas.

1 Location 3 Construction: 3.1 time 3.2 cost
2 Type of building 4 Opening

The Sydney Opera House

The Sydney Opera House is one of the most famous architectural wonders of the modern world. Instantly recognizable both for its roof shells and its impressive location in Sydney Harbour, it has become one of the best known images of Australia.

Situated close to Sydney Harbour Bridge, this large performing arts centre was started in 1959 and completed in 1973. After a competition to choose the design, the Danish architect Jorn Utzon was chosen. The Opera House includes five theatres, five rehearsal studios, two main halls, four restaurants, six bars, and several shops.

The construction of the Opera House was fairly controversial as the final cost of the building was much higher than predicted. It was expected to cost $7 million, but in fact, the final cost was $102 million. This was due to difficult weather conditions, problems with the structural design, and changes in the contract. The remarkable roof shells were also difficult to construct. Furthermore, the construction took longer than planned. Completion of the building was initially expected in four years, in 1963. Unfortunately, because of the many problems and changes which were necessary in the design, the building was not completed until ten years later, in 1973.

It was inaugurated by Queen Elizabeth II on 20 October 1973, and millions of people attended the ceremony. The event was televised, and included a fireworks display and a classical music performance.

Writing a summary

7 Write a summary of the text *The Sydney Opera House* (100–120 words). Use structures from *Language for Writing* on page 56.

REVIEW

1 Read the article and answer the questions.

1 What was Skylab and why was it built?
2 When and how many times was Skylab in operation?
3 What happened during the first mission?
4 What kind of research was done?
5 Why and when did it crash-land?

Skylab

Skylab was the first space station **launched** into **orbit** around the Earth. It was designed to prove that man could spend long periods of time in space, and to make observations of the **solar** system which were not possible from the Earth. It was first launched on 14 May 1973, but during the launch it **sustained** severe damage. Helped by ground control, the **crew** managed   5
to repair this damage during a spacewalk, and the **mission** continued. In total, there were three Skylab missions between 1973 and 1975, during which time many scientific studies were carried out. These included medical experiments, investigations into **gravitational** effects, and solar observations. The missions proved that man could function effectively in space for periods of up to 84 days. In 1975 Skylab was abandoned and left to orbit the Earth. It was   10
expected to remain in orbit for ten years, but atmospheric changes pulled it back to Earth. It crash-landed in Australia in 1979, spreading its **debris** over a large area.

2 Guess the meaning of the words in bold in the text. Complete the table.

word	part of speech	your guess
launched	verb	to send into the sky

3 Underline the main clause in the sentences.

1 Helped by ground control, the crew managed to repair this damage during a spacewalk, and the mission continued.

2 In total, there were three Skylab missions between 1973 and 1975, during which time many scientific studies were carried out.

3 It crash-landed in Australia in 1979, spreading its debris over a large area.

4 What do the pronouns refer to? Look back at the article and complete the table.

pronoun	refers to
It (line 2)	_____
which (line 4)	_____
it (line 5)	_____
These (line 8)	_____
its (line 12)	_____

5 Write a summary of the text in one or two sentences.

6 Complete the table with the correct parts of speech for each word. Mark the stressed syllables.

verb	noun	adjective	adverb
			complėtely
di̇ffer			
	observȧtion		
prove			
	sci̇ence		
succeėd			

8 Olympic business

READING The Olympic Games

1 Discuss the questions with a partner.

1 What do the five rings in the symbol of the Olympic Games represent?
2 Do you enjoy watching the Olympics?
3 If so, which sports do you watch?
4 Why do cities want to host the Olympics?

2 Skim the text. Match paragraphs A–G with their content 1–5.

1 ☐ Conclusion
2 ☐ Arguments against hosting the Games
3 ☐ Introduction
4 ☐ ☐ ☐ Arguments for hosting the Games and information about costs
5 ☐ Selection requirements

3 Find the words and phrases 1–11 in bold in the text. Match them with their meanings a–k.

Barcelona'92

© 1988 COOB'92, S.A All rights reserved TM

word		meaning
1 ☐ host		a enough for what you need
2 ☐ facilities		b people or organizations that help to pay for a special event
3 ☐ adequate		c food, drink, and entertainment given to visitors
4 ☐ bid		d permission to show something on TV, etc.
5 ☐ sponsors		e services, buildings, or pieces of equipment provided for people to use
6 ☐ broadcasting rights		f an action which stops something continuing
7 ☐ vigilance		g to continue for a period of time
8 ☐ manpower		h an effort or attempt to obtain something
9 ☐ hospitality		i to provide the space and other necessary things for an event, etc.
10 ☐ last		j the act of watching and looking out for danger
11 ☐ disruption		k the people that you need to do a particular job

4 Scan the text and answer the questions.

1 Which two groups of people can use the accommodation built for the Olympic Games afterwards?
2 What three ways of funding the Olympics, besides taxes, are mentioned?
3 How might the Games affect the daily lives of ordinary people?

5 Read the text intensively and complete the notes in the diagram for the advantages and disadvantages of hosting the Games.

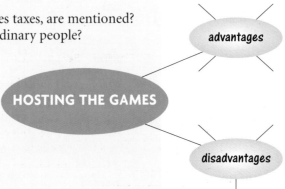

advantages

HOSTING THE GAMES

disadvantages

Hosting the Olympics

A Sport plays a significant part in the everyday lives of people around the world. This is true not only for those who take part, but also for those who merely watch. Large sports events have become great entertainment, and at the same time huge business. Today, the Olympic Games are one of the most popular and most watched events in the world. Every four years many countries enter the fierce competition to **host** the Games. Why do they do this? What are the advantages and disadvantages of hosting such an event?

B In order to select which city or state will host the Olympics, the International Olympic Committee asks several fundamental questions. Are the sports **facilities adequate**? Is there enough accommodation? Is the transport system efficient and sufficient? How will the event be funded? What are the security arrangements? In making a **bid** for the Olympics, every host city addresses these questions.

C A world-class event demands world-class facilities from the host city, and any which do not already exist will have to be built. These will remain for the local population to enjoy after the Games are over. An example of this is the accommodation which will have to be built, not only for the athletes in their Olympic village, but also for the visitors. Later this can be turned into permanent accommodation for tourists and students. The transport system must also be taken into consideration. Hosting the Olympics means having an effective wide-reaching system, which is necessary to carry people safely and quickly to their destinations. Such a transport system is a great advantage for any city and will be in place for many years to come.

D Funding any great event is an expensive business, but many companies fiercely compete to become **sponsors** of such global events as it is an ideal opportunity for advertising. This means that advertising revenues can easily cover a large proportion of the costs involved. In addition, the **broadcasting rights** can be a source of finance. According to Lee (2006), the national American TV company NBC paid $3.5 billion to transmit the Olympic Games between 2000 and 2008.

E Another consideration is employment. Hosting an event of worldwide importance requires increased **vigilance**, which is expensive in terms of technology and **manpower**. High-tech video cameras are already common in most of our big cities today, and increasing the manpower necessary to guarantee the safety of all concerned provides valuable employment opportunities. Indeed, the organization of such an event gives rise to a large number of jobs in a variety of sectors including security, catering, and **hospitality**.

F However, there are disadvantages to holding the Games. Although jobs will be created, many of these are not permanent and only **last** for the period of the construction or the Games themselves, and many are unskilled. In addition, the increased number of visitors to the area can cause serious **disruption** to the daily lives of ordinary citizens. The local inhabitants may also have to face tax increases, as not all the funding will come from sponsorship or advertising.

G In conclusion, although there are disadvantages to holding the Olympic Games, it is generally agreed that the host city gains overall in terms of improvements in facilities and infrastructure. But this is not all. According to Stevenson (1997), "The Olympics make other people aware of your country and what's there. It's a way to make a statement to the world that your community is a destination" (p.236). Not only do the improved facilities remain after the Games have gone, but the city also becomes a significant place in its own right.

(606 words)

Lee, J. K. Marketing and promotion of the Olympic Games. *The Sport Journal, 18*. Retrieved September 15, 2006, from http://www.thesportjournal.org/2005Journal/Vol8-No3/

Stevenson, D. (1997). Olympic arts: Sydney 2000 and the cultural Olympiad. *International Review for the Sociology of Sport, 32(2)*, 227–238.

6 Complete the notes for the remaining information. **Read Study Skill**

1 **Requirements**	2 **Funding**
1.1 Sports facilities	2.1 _____
1.2 Accommodation	2.2 _____
1.3 _____	2.3 _____
1.4 _____	3 **Conclusion**
1.5 _____	3.1 _____
	3.2 _____

STUDY SKILL Making notes

When you read, keep a record of what you have read. There are different methods of note-taking, for example, a diagram, a table, and headings and numbers. Choose a method you prefer.

Two Olympic bids

7 Skim the texts. What kind of texts are they? What information do they give you?

To: COULSON, Bob
Cc:
Subject: Rockley's bid for Winter Olympics

Dear Bob,

Here's the information you asked for about the city of Rockley's bid for the Winter Olympic Games.

Overall budget is now $3.5 billion. This includes $650 m for capital costs (upgrading existing facilities and building new ones). I've heard that the improvements to the transport system will cost $700 m, and Rockley has allowed $650 m for overheads and unexpected costs. They estimate that the operating costs will be $1.5 billion.

I hope that gives you what you need!

Best wishes,

Keith

To: RICHARDSON, Keith
Cc:
Subject: Rockley's bid for Winter Olympics

Dear Keith,

Thanks for your mail and the information about the bid. I still don't see how Rockley intends to fund this. Do you have any details?

Best

Bob

To: COULSON, Bob
Cc:
Subject: Rockley's bid for Winter Olympics

Dear Bob,

Yes, I do know about the funding.

The national government will provide $1.6 billion. The regional government has promised to give $360 m and Rockley itself will raise $140 m. The rest of the money will come from ticket sales ($150 m), TV broadcasting rights (this is estimated at $750 m), and sponsorship ($500 m is the figure they give).

Best wishes,

Keith

8 Read the texts intensively and complete the notes in the table for Rockley.

Bids for the Winter Olympic Games in dollars	Rockley	Woodville
overall budget		3.2 billion
capital costs		700 million
operating costs		1.4 billion
transport upgrade		600 million
overheads & unexpected costs		500 million
government funding		200 million
regional funding		200 million
city funding		800 million
TV rights		900 million
ticket sales		300 million
sponsorship		100 million

9 Look at the bid in the table above from another city, Woodville. Answer the questions.

1 What are the major differences between the two bids?
2 Which bid is more realistic, and why?

RESEARCH Crediting sources (2)

1 `Read Study Skill` Read the text and underline the references which are acknowledged.

> In recent years sport has become big business with vast sums of money involved. It has been claimed that America spent $24 billion on sports marketing in 2004 (Matache, 2005). Large sporting events such as the World Cup and the Olympics receive lucrative television contracts which enable them to fund their events. The TV networks pay for these contracts with money from companies who advertise during these televised events. The cost of advertising on TV varies, and it is difficult to calculate the true amount. However, it has been claimed that "a prime time 30-second slot on Australian TV costs $400,000." (Sinden, 2004, p. 487). Companies will also use sports personalities to advertise their products. For the sports personality, it is an easy way to increase their income. One example of this is Tiger Woods, who earned $75 million in 2005 off the golf course.

2 Complete the text, using the information in the references.

> Although many cities compete to host large sports events such as the World Cup or the Grand Prix, many of them are left with large debts after the event is over. [1]_____ (2003) claims that "estimates for the costs are always inferior to the actual needs" (p. 67). There are various reasons for this, but according to Vince (2006), few organizers take into consideration the real rate of inflation, and this results in large debts. These debts can prove to be long lasting. Smallridge [2]_____ argues "remaining debts can stay with a host city for many decades" [3]_____. Nevertheless, cities still compete to hold the Games, seeing them as advantageous for the community.
>
> ---
>
> Haggeg, K. F. (2003). *Host cities of the Olympics*. Canberra: Highlight Press.
> Vince, F. T. (2006). Inflation in costing estimates. *Accountancy Review, 5,* 45.
> Smallridge, E. C. (2006). Hosting the Olympics. What remains? *The Journal of Accounts, 6,* 52.
>   Retrieved January 2, 2006, from http://www.thejournalofaccounts.com

3 `Read Study Skill` Rewrite the following direct quotations with the correct punctuation.

1 according to Woodbridge 2004 p23 football is bigger business than selling food
   According to Woodbridge (2004), "football is bigger business than selling food" (p.23).

2 Khalil 2003 claims hosting large events usually leaves the host city with large bills p54

3 as Li Chung wrote 1999 the opportunity for development is considerable p71

4 Neal 2001 said transport upgrades are inevitable p268

STUDY SKILL
Avoiding plagiarism (3)

Sometimes you need to quote sources in your writing.
For direct quotations, that is, the author's exact words, give:

- name of author
- date of publication
- page number

He stated, "The quality of the bids has never been higher" (Sinden, 2004, p. 487).

Sinden (2004) stated that "the quality of the bids has never been higher" (p. 487).

For indirect quotations give:

- name of author
- date of publication

He argued that the next Games should be held in Africa (Jones, 2005).

Jones (2005) argued that the next Games should be held in Africa.

Remember to include a complete reference in the list of references or bibliography (see Study Skill p56).

STUDY SKILL
Avoiding plagiarism (4)

When you quote directly from a source, you must use quotation marks. For example:
Carter (2006) believes, "The benefits to a city of holding the Olympics will always outweigh the disadvantages" (p. 10).
Brown (2004) argues that "the high cost of the Games will fall on the taxpayer" (p. 25).

When you quote indirectly, do not use quotation marks. For example:
Cox (2006) suggested that without adequate sponsorship, the Games could not take place.

LANGUAGE FOR WRITING Expressing contrast

1 Look at the sentences from the text on page 61. Underline the words of contrast.

   1 … However, there are disadvantages to holding the Games.
   2 … although there are disadvantages to holding the Olympic Games, it is generally agreed that the host city gains overall in terms of improvements in facilities and infrastructure.

2 Read the rules. Match 1–4 with a–d to make complete sentences. Make a note of the punctuation used with each word or phrase of contrast.

1 ☐ In spite of the government estimating the total cost of the Games to be 3.2 billion dollars,	a the crowds were enormous.
2 ☐ Forty per cent of the population watched the final,	b Nevertheless, she succeeded in breaking the world record.
3 ☐ Despite the cold weather,	c even though it was televised in the middle of the night.
4 ☐ The world champion had had an injury for two months.	d the actual cost was considerably higher.

> ### RULES Contrast
>
> Use words and phrases of contrast, for example, **however**, **although**, **nevertheless**, **despite**, to link surprising, contrasting, or unexpected information.
>
> **However** and **nevertheless** introduce a second sentence which contrasts with the first.
>
> *The department announced there would be exams twice a year. However, not everyone agreed with their decision.*
> *The city put together an extremely good bid for the Games. Nevertheless, they were unsuccessful.*
>
> **Although** and **even though** introduce a clause which contrasts with the main clause. The main clause says something surprising or unexpected.
>
> *Although/Even though jobs will be created, many of these are not permanent.*
>
> **Despite** and **In spite of** are similar in meaning to **although**. They are used with a noun or -*ing* form of the verb.
>
> *In spite of earning money through advertising, the athletes claimed they were underpaid.*
> *Thousands of spectators attended the match despite the bad weather.*
>
> Note the use of punctuation in the sentences.

however
although
nevertheless
even though
despite
in spite of

3 Link each pair of sentences, using the words or phrases in brackets.

   1 It costs a huge amount of money to fund the Games.
     Many cities compete to hold them.   (although)
   2 The Olympic Organizing Committee raised a large amount of money to fund the Games.
     Huge debts remained after the Games.   (despite)
   3 The majority of the population were in favour of hosting the event.
     There was opposition to the tax increases.   (nevertheless)
   4 The football club had raised considerable sums of money through advertising.
     It did not have sufficient funds to construct a new stadium.   (in spite of)
   5 The team had not played together for very long.
     They won the game.   (however)
   6 The event was broadcast on national television.
     Ten per cent of the population were unaware it was taking place.
     (even though)

WRITING A permanent site for the Olympics

1 You are going to write an essay with the title *Should the Olympics have a permanent home?* (250–300 words). Plan your essay.

- Brainstorm ideas (see Study Skill p25).
- Make notes, using a method of your choice (see Study Skill p61).
- Develop the essay title into a thesis statement (see Study Skill p32).
- Select and organize your notes into arguments *for* and *against* your thesis statement (see Study Skill p41).

2 Read the quotations. Select two or more which support your arguments in exercise 1.

> 1 **"Adopting a permanent site would avoid any international disagreements between countries."**
> Kinghorn, J. E. (2006). Arguing for a permanent site. *Journal of International Sport, 54*, 341–352.
>
> 2 **"The vast majority of people questioned preferred the Olympics to be held in a different city every four years."**
> Jenkins, L. P. (2007). Popularity issues and the Games. *The New Review of International Events, 4*, 63–74.
>
> 3 **"The facilities at a permanent site could be reused every four years. Between Games, they would serve as international training facilities."**
> *A permanent home?* Retrieved May 31, 2006, from http://www.gamestoday.com
>
> 4 **"Awarding the Games permanently to Greece would recognize the historical origins."**
> Bailey, P. (2006, August 31). A permanent home for the Olympics. *The Daily Chronicle*. p. 10.
>
> 5 **"No city welcomes the enormous disruption every four years."**
> Cooper, H. S. (2005). Take the Games elsewhere. *Review of Event Management, 11*, 85–98.
>
> 6 **"Deciding on a permanent home for the Olympics would end the expensive process of selecting a host city every four years."**
> Macklin, S. M. (2004). *The Olympic Games: a short history*. Hartford: Wollings Press.
>
> 7 **"A permanent site would provide an international centre for sport."**
> Dominguez, L. M. Retrieved January 23, 2007, from http://www.internationalsport.com.au/articles/.html
>
> 8 **"A permanent site would give unfair financial advantages to the host city."**
> Roberts, T. K. (2006). *The Olympic sites*. Hong Kong: Marina Press.
>
> 9 **"The Games are a serial financial burden for any city."**
> Jolly, M. B. (2007). Hosting the Games. *Journal of Sport Today, 12*, 13–27.

Writing a discursive essay

3 Using your notes and quotations, write:

- the introductory paragraph (see Study Skill p32)
- the body paragraphs (see Study Skill p16)
- a concluding paragraph (see Study Skill p33)

4 Check your essay for:

- content, organization, and style (see Study Skills p33 and p48), making sure you have credited any sources
- mistakes in grammar, punctuation, spelling, and sentence structure (see Study Skills p9 and p11)

5 Write out the final corrected version of your essay. `Read Study Skill`

STUDY SKILL Process writing

Essay writing involves the following stages:

- brainstorming and making notes
- developing a thesis statement
- selecting and organizing notes appropriately
- including quotations which support your arguments
- writing the essay
- checking the essay

VOCABULARY DEVELOPMENT Synonyms

1 **Read Study Skill** Look at sentences a–d for each question. In one of the sentences the word in italics is wrong. Find the sentence and cross it out. Use a dictionary to help.

1 a The athlete *earned* the respect of his team.
  b The athlete *gained* the respect of his team.
  c The football player *earned* over one million euros last year.
  d The football player ~~gained~~ over one million euros last year.

2 a The state promised to provide the necessary *finance*.
  b The state promised to provide the necessary *money*.
  c The student borrowed the *finance* to fund his studies.
  d The student borrowed the *money* to fund his studies.

3 a The winner *raised* his arm to salute the spectators.
  b The winner *increased* his arm to salute the spectators.
  c Taxes will be *raised* to pay for the new transport system.
  d Taxes will be *increased* to pay for the new transport system.

2 Complete the sentences with the correct form of a word from the box. Compare your answers with a partner.

sponsor   raise   increase   gain   earn   support

1 The multinational company agreed to _____ the event by providing equipment for the teams.
2 The funds will be _____ by inviting people to invest in the company.
3 What will the city _____ from holding the Olympics?
4 The price of travelling on public transport has _____ by two per cent this year.
5 Athletes often _____ extra money only from sponsorship.
6 The injured player walked off the pitch, _____ by his coach.

Words often have synonyms or near synonyms. However, you cannot always use synonyms in every context. Use a dictionary to check whether a word is correct for a particular context. For example:

The TV programme was broadcast/transmitted all over the world.

Some illnesses are ~~broadcast~~/transmitted by insects.

Antonyms

3 **Read Study Skill** Cross out the incorrect antonym in brackets for the word in italics. Use a dictionary to help.

1 There are an *odd* number of players on each team. (even/normal)
2 The event was planned to start at an *odd* time of day. (even/normal)
3 There is a *strong* possibility that the match will be broadcast on TV. (weak/slight)
4 The organizer gave a *strong* argument for hosting the event next year. (weak/slight)

4 Choose the correct antonym in brackets for the word in italics.

1 The knife was very *sharp*. (dull/blunt)
2 The vaccination caused a *sharp* pain in the patient's arm. (dull/blunt)
3 *Voluntary* redundancy is quite common in many companies. (compulsory/paid)
4 The charity is looking for people to do *voluntary* work. (compulsory/paid)
5 The student spoke in a *soft* voice. (loud/hard)
6 The ground was too *soft* to camp on. (loud/hard)

STUDY SKILL Antonyms

An antonym is a word with the opposite meaning to another word, e.g. *huge* ≠ *tiny*.

You cannot always use antonyms in every context. Use a dictionary to check. For example:

*The student's results were very **poor** this term.* (~~wealthy~~/good)

*The committee's decision depends on how **poor** the city is.* (wealthy/~~good~~)

REVIEW

1 Read the text. Make notes about…

  1 where the World Cup has been held   3 the television audiences
  2 which countries have won it

The World Cup

The World Cup is an international football competition which is held every four years. One of the most popular events in the world, the first competition took place in 1930 in Uruguay.

Each time there is a different host country, although until 2002, when it took place in Korea and Japan, it was always held in Europe and the Americas. In 2010 it is being held in Africa for the first time.

Only seven countries have ever won the World Cup. Brazil has been the most successful over the years, winning five times. Italy is in second place, having won four times, and Germany has won three times. Argentina and Uruguay have both won twice, and France and England once.

The World Cup was first broadcast on television in 1954 and is now the most popular televised sporting event in the world. It has been reported that <u>more spectators watch the event than the Olympic Games</u> (Foster, 1997). The audience of the 2002 World Cup held in Korea and Japan was estimated to be almost 30 billion. According to FIFA (2006), the international governing body of football, <u>1.1 billion people watched the final match of this tournament</u>. Broadcasting this event resulted in 41,100 hours of football on TV across the world. Clearly, the World Cup matches attract huge audiences, but even the draws, which decide the distribution of teams into groups, are widely viewed. The 2006 World Cup draw was, as Brown (2006) reported, <u>seen by 300 million people</u>.

2 Rewrite the underlined indirect quotations as direct quotations with the correct punctuation.

3 Rewrite the sources in the correct APA style.

  a 2002 FIFA World Cup TV Coverage. Retrieved May 13, 2006 from www.fifa.com/en/marketing/concept/ondex.
  b Smallridge, E.C. (2006) Hosting the Olympics. What remains? Retrieved January 2, 2006, from http://www.thejournalofaccounts.com
  c "Watching sports events" by Jeremy Mark Foster 1997. Journal of Televised Events 23. 32–45.
  d Nora Brown. "Football and television" International Review of Media 2006. 65. 21–34

4 Link the sentences, using the words in brackets.

  1 The committee only met on one occasion. It organized the event very well. (despite)
  2 The weather was very hot. The athlete broke the world record. (although)
  3 The tickets for the match were very expensive. All the tickets were sold within a few hours. (however)
  4 The funds for the event were sufficient. The city was not chosen. (in spite of)
  5 The chairman was appointed for four years. He resigned after six months. (nevertheless)

5 Choose the correct synonym in brackets for the words in italics.

  1 a The cafeteria was too noisy to *hold* a conversation in. (host/have)
      b Rockley is *holding* the Winter Games next year. (hosting/having)
  2 a The company is going to *hire* two new managers. (employ/rent)
      b When they arrived at the airport, they *hired* a car. (employed/rented)
  3 a The *plan* of the city indicated all the major sites of interest. (map/arrangements)
      b The *plans* for the conference were changed at the last minute. (maps/arrangements)
  4 a *Full* details of the programme are available on the website. (complete/busy).
      b The professor cannot see you tomorrow as he has a very *full* day. (complete/busy).

9 Trends

READING SKILLS Understanding visual information: graphics • Interpreting data
LANGUAGE FOR WRITING Language for describing graphs, charts, and statistics
WRITING SKILLS Using graphs to present data • Writing a report using visual information
VOCABULARY DEVELOPMENT Prefixes

READING Work

1 Discuss the questions with a partner.

  1 Name some of the sectors of employment. **agriculture, ...**
  2 Which sectors employ the most people in your country?
  3 Has the number of employees in the different sectors changed in recent years?
  4 Which sector would you like to work in?

2 **Read Study Skill** Survey the text *Work trends* on page 69. Which graphic is …

  1 a line graph?
  2 a bar chart?
  3 a pie chart?

3 Skim the title, text, and graphics. Answer the questions.

  1 What do the graphics show?
  2 How are they different?
  3 What do you notice about the number of people employed in agriculture and services in 2005?
  4 In which sector did the number of jobs rise between 1995 and 2005?
  5 How has the number of people working in IT changed?

STUDY SKILL
Understanding visual information: graphics

Academic texts often contain statistics in the form of graphs or charts.

  ■ **Line graphs** show specific trends in data, often on a time line.
  ■ **Bar charts** illustrate comparisons in trends.
  ■ **Pie charts** compare percentages of a whole piece of data.

Referring to these as you read helps you understand the text.

  ■ Skim the titles of the graphics to get a general idea.
  ■ Look at the graphics and ask yourself some general questions, e.g. *What is the overall picture? Are there any unexpected points?*
  ■ As you read the text, refer to the appropriate graphics.

---

4 Read the text and look at the graphics. Answer the questions.

  1 Why has there been a decrease in the number of jobs in the textile industry?
  2 What has happened to the number of jobs in the industrial sector?
  3 What two things do you learn about employment trends in South-East Asia?
  4 What happened to employment in IT in the 1990s?
  5 How have developments in ICTs affected the way work is done?

5 Underline the correct words in italics to complete the sentences, using information from the text and figures 1–3.

  1 There were *almost as many/not nearly as many* people working in industry as in agriculture in 2005.
  2 Between 1995 and 2005 there was a *slight/substantial* decrease in jobs in industry.
  3 In 1998 there were *considerably/marginally* more jobs in IT than in 1992.
  4 *Five per cent/A tenth* of all jobs will be in ICTs in the future.
  5 Economists predict there will be *an increase/a decrease* in the number of people working in industry in the future.

Work trends

The type of work which people do is constantly changing as man develops and modifies his way of living. One hundred years ago, the vast majority of people worked in agriculture, but now less than half the world's population do so. In fact, in only ten years major changes have been seen in the percentage of the workforce employed in various sectors.

Figure 1 shows the overall distribution of jobs in the three major sectors in 2005: agriculture, industry, and services. It can be seen that almost the same percentage of people worked in services as in agriculture, whereas only around 20% were employed in industry. In the ten years leading up to 2005, substantial changes in employment took place, reflecting changes in technology and lifestyle.

As Figure 2 illustrates, a significant change took place in the agricultural sector. In 1995 43% of the world's workforce was employed in agriculture; by 2005 this number had fallen to 40%. The largest decline was in South-East Asia and the Pacific, where the figures dropped by 12%.

Similarly, in industry the workforce fell by two per cent globally. Manufacturing was the largest sub-sector of industry to be affected. However, these figures represent only an overall picture, as some countries saw industrial employment actually rise by one per cent. This was particularly noticeable in certain South-East Asian countries, where low wages and fast industrialization have enabled countries like China to become world leaders in manufacturing. In other sub-sectors of industry such as textiles, the global workforce dropped from 14.5 million in 1990 to 13 million in 2000, as increasing automation reduced the number of employees needed.

However, one sector saw an increase. The service sector employed 34% of the workforce in 1995, but by 2005 this had risen to 39%. This extremely varied sector includes the retail trade, tourist-related services such as hotels and restaurants, as well as transport, communications, finance, property, research and development, education, and health care. The largest developments were seen in the new Information and Communications Technologies (ICTs), which have grown rapidly since the 1990s. The developments in ICTs have had a huge impact on jobs in all sectors, as computer technology has radically affected the way in which work is done. The means of production, distribution, and communication have all been transformed. The number of jobs in IT as a percentage of all jobs in the service sector is represented in Figure 3.

Although there was a slight drop in the numbers of jobs in IT in the mid-1990s due to a recession, the overall trend was upward. As technology spreads across the world, this rise in jobs will continue. It is estimated that one in twenty new jobs will be in ICTs in the future.

Economists predict that these overall tendencies will continue. There will be a further increase in service-sector employment, and in particular in ICTs, but health care and education will also benefit from more jobs. At the same time, fewer people will be employed in industry and agriculture.

(503 words)

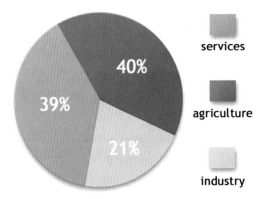

Figure 1 Percentage of the global workforce in the major sectors in 2005

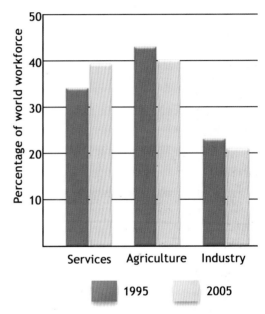

Figure 2 Sectors of global employment in 1995 and 2005

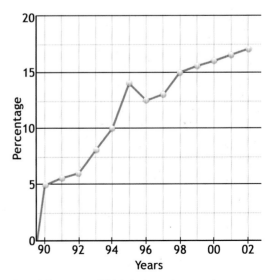

Figure 3 Percentage of IT jobs in the service sector between 1990 and 2002

Trends in education

6 Skim Figure 4. What was the most popular subject for women and the least popular subject for men in both years?

subject	2000–2001		2006–2007	
	men	women	men	women
arts	495	989	560	1020
medicine & dentistry	154	186	130	230
information technology	108	72	143	86
engineering & technology	245	119	264	123
law	300	103	358	196
economics & commerce	461	466	467	406

Figure 4: Enrolment statistics at Coral University

7 **Read Study Skill** Look at Figure 4 in detail. Read the text about changing trends at Coral University. Complete paragraphs B and C with words and phrases from the box.

just over	nearly	the same	just under	three-quarters	twice as many

Changing trends

A There has been an overall rise in the numbers of students enrolling in higher education in the last twenty years. The subjects chosen by students reflect trends in the job market as well as changes in the students' fields of interest and research.

B Figure 4 shows the numbers of students enrolled at Coral University for the years 2000–2001 and 2006–2007, according to subjects studied. For the academic year 2000–2001, the most popular subjects for both men and women were in the arts, with [1]_____ 500 men and approximately [2]_____ women studying these subjects. In economics and commerce the numbers of men and women were almost [3]_____. However, engineering and technology were more popular with male students, with only 119 women, compared with 245 men choosing these subjects. Information technology was also more popular with men, with 108 male and 72 female students, and in law just under [4]_____ of the total number were men.

C The academic year 2006–2007 saw a general increase in student numbers, as most faculties registered a rise in enrolments. For example, the number of men studying IT rose from 108 in 2000 to [5]_____ 140 in 2006, and numbers studying law rose to over 350 men and [6]_____ 200 women. There were some decreases. The number of men studying medicine and dentistry dropped to 130, and the number of women studying economics and commerce also fell by 60, to 406.

D It is predicted that this increase in student numbers and changing trends in subject choice will continue over the coming years. Universities will expand to receive these growing numbers, and new faculties will open.

the majority
the same as
almost
approximately
just under
just over

LANGUAGE FOR WRITING
Language for describing graphs, charts, and statistics

1 Match a type of graph 1–3 with a description a–c (see Study Skill p68).

1 ☐ The bar chart shows/illustrates	a the percentage of graduates working in different sectors.
2 ☐ The line graph shows/illustrates	b the number of graduates who work in IT in different countries of the world.
3 ☐ The pie chart compares	c the number of students in New Zealand between 1990 and 2005.

2 Write the words from the box in the table.

> go up   soar   plummet   decline   increase   rocket
> level out   stabilize   fluctuate   go down   grow
> plunge   reach a peak   decrease

rise	fall	stay the same	change frequently	peak

3 Complete the table with the adjective + noun phrases.

verb + adverb	adjective + noun
rose dramatically	a dramatic rise
fell substantially	
increased considerably	
dropped slightly	
decreased noticeably	
grew marginally	
declined steadily	

4 Which adjectives and adverbs in exercise 3 describe a large change and which describe a small change?

substantially/substantial = a large change

5 Correct the wrong information in the description of each graph.

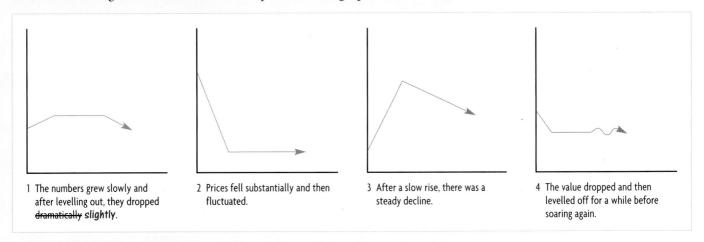

1 The numbers grew slowly and after levelling out, they dropped ~~dramatically~~ **slightly**.

2 Prices fell substantially and then fluctuated.

3 After a slow rise, there was a steady decline.

4 The value dropped and then levelled off for a while before soaring again.

6 Replace the underlined words or phrases with the equivalent from the box.

| 90% of | 47% | 70% of | nearly two-thirds | a quarter |

1 <u>Seven in ten</u> students live in university accommodation.
2 <u>25%</u> of arts graduates work in education.
3 <u>Nine out of ten</u> textile workers are women.
4 <u>64%</u> of jobs in the textile industry are in South-East Asia.
5 <u>Almost half</u> of office workers travel more than 30 minutes to reach their work.

7 Read paragraph C from the text *Changing trends* on page 70. Underline the nouns and verbs which refer to changes. Circle the prepositions which go with them.

> **C** The academic year 2006–2007 saw a general increase in student numbers, as most faculties registered a rise in enrolments. For example, the number of men studying IT rose from 108 in 2000 to just over 140 in 2006, and numbers studying law rose to over 350 men and just under 200 women. There were some decreases. The number of men studying medicine and dentistry dropped to 130, and the number of women studying economics and commerce also fell by 60, to 406.

8 Look at the graph in figure 5 and complete the gaps in the text with a preposition from the box.

| to | from | to | of | by | to | in |

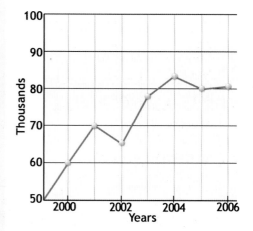

Figure 5 The number of people employed in education, health, and social services between 2000 and 2006

> There was a general increase ¹_____ the number of people employed in education, health, and social services between 2000 and 2006. Between 2000 and 2001, the numbers rose ²_____ 70,000, but there was a slight drop ³_____ 5,000 the following year. Numbers rose again in 2003 ⁴_____ 78,000. In 2004 the workforce increased ⁵_____ 5,000 and then dropped slightly ⁶_____ 83,000 ⁷_____ 80,000 in 2005. This figure remained almost the same in 2006.

WRITING Population trends

1 Discuss the questions about your country with a partner.

1 In what ways is the population changing?
2 Are there more young people than people over 60?
3 What are the percentages of men and women?

2 Decide which type of graph would be best for showing 1–3 (see Study Skill page 68).

1 changes in the number of people under 20 in a country between 1995 and 2005
2 the percentage of undergraduates and graduate students in a particular university
3 the number of men and women who worked in information technology between 1998 and 2006

3 Decide which data in Tables 1–4 you would use in a report on the distribution of the world's population by age.

Table 1: Total world population by age in millions in 2002 and 2025

age	2002	2025
total	6,227,966	7,833,456
0–4	605,138	625,701
5–9	596,123	626,510
10–14	607,387	623,151
15–19	580,448	604,049
20–44	2,352,784	2,819,888
45–64	1,045,771	1,700,854
65–79	363,177	668,912
Over 80	77,138	164,400

Table 2: Percentage global distribution of males by age in 2004

	under 15	15–64	over 65
the world	29.1	64.6	6.3
Africa	42.2	54.8	3
Asia	28.6	65.7	5.7
Europe	17.2	70.1	12.7

Table 3: Percentage global distribution of females by age in 2004

	under 15	15–64	over 65
the world	27.9	63.8	8.3
Africa	41.1	55.1	3.7
Asia	27.9	65.1	7.0
Europe	15.1	66.3	18.5

Table 4: Percentage of students employed in part-time work

year	percentage
2002	21
2003	31
2004	26
2005	28

4 **Read Study Skill** Decide how you would present the data you have chosen from exercise 3. Draw a graph or chart.

STUDY SKILL Using graphs to present data

In your writing present statistical and numerical data in a graphic form for clarity. Refer to the graphics and describe the overall patterns rather than all the statistics in detail.

---

5 Look at the graphics. Answer the questions.
1 What are the main trends?
2 Are there any surprising rises or falls?

Writing a report using visual information

6 Plan your report for exercise 3. Refer back to the *Language for Writing* on page 71.

7 Write a report (150–200 words).

VOCABULARY DEVELOPMENT Word-building (2)

STUDY SKILL Prefixes

Prefixes are a letter or a group of letters which you add at the beginning of a word. Understanding the meaning of a prefix will help you understand the word. For example:

bio – means *connected with living things or human life*, e.g. ***bio**chemistry*

The negative or antonym of some words is formed with a prefix. For example:

*necessary ≠ **un**necessary*
*relevant ≠ **ir**relevant*

1 **Read Study Skill** Use a dictionary to check the meaning of the words in italics. Underline the prefixes. Write the prefixes and the words in the correct place in the table.

1 The students are learning English in a *multilingual* class.
having or using several different languages
2 Art critics were invited to a *preview* of the new exhibition.
3 Plants use the process of *photosynthesis* to make food.
4 Many professions require *postgraduate* qualifications.
5 Remember to *reread* your essay before you hand it in.
6 Many companies have their own *intranet* system.
7 *Biochemistry* is the study of the chemistry of living things.
8 Bacteria and fungi are *microorganisms.*
9 In a marathon the athletes run over 42 *kilometres.*
10 The new *monorail* train runs above the ground.
11 An *international* conference is being held in July.
12 The two countries were involved in *bilateral* trade talks.

number	size	time	place	substance	negatives/antonyms
poly- e.g. polyunsaturated multi- e.g. multilingual	*nano-* e.g. nanogram	*ante-* e.g. antecedent	*sub-* e.g. subtitles	*hydro-* e.g. hydroelectric	*un-* e.g. unsuitable

2 Underline the negative adjectives in the sentences. Add the prefixes and adjectives to the table in exercise 1.

1 The patient was suffering from an irregular heartbeat.
2 The public transport system was described as inefficient.
3 The painting was an imperfect copy of the original.
4 The student's work was often disorganized.
5 The candidate was unsuitable for the job.
6 The doctor's handwriting was illegible.

3 Complete the sentences, using a form of the word in brackets and a suitable prefix.

1 The instrument could measure one billionth of a second, or a ____________, accurately. (second)
2 The scientists required a ____________ (marine) to explore the bottom of the sea.
3 A ____________ is a light boat with an engine and a flat bottom which can travel over the surface of the water. (plane)
4 ____________ is the time in history before events were written down. (history)
5 The bus service is completely ____________. I had to wait 30 minutes for a bus. (reliable)
6 Most people in the city are ____________, speaking both French and German. (lingual)

poly-
nano-
ante-
hydro-
sub-
un-

REVIEW

1 Draw an appropriate graphic to represent the data in table 5.

Table 5: Graduate employment destinations from Woodville University in 1998 and 2004 in percentages		
sector	**1998**	**2004**
banking & insurance	9	5
retail	15	6
ICT	4	7
health & social work	10	13
education & research	19	24
media	3	5
public services	8	10
manufacturing	14	13
consultancy	10	9
financial & legal	4	6
other	4	2

2 Write a description of the graphic you have drawn in exercise 1.

3 Add a prefix to the word in brackets to match the definition.
1 To program a piece of electrical equipment in advance. (set)
2 A thousand grams. (gram)
3 Against the law. (legal)
4 To take an exam again. (take)
5 Only speaking one language. (lingual)

4 **Read Study Skill** Underline the stem of the words in italics.
1 The seats in the arena were rather *uncomfortable*.
2 The statistics were *inaccurately* collected.
3 The physicists were surprised by the *reappearance* of the star in the sky.
4 At first glance the two essays were *indistinguishable*.
5 Research scientists are encouraged to work on *interdisciplinary* projects.

5 Write a definition for the composite word in italics.
1 *Unquestionably*, the greatest change in recent years has been the growth in the population.

   Without question

2 The results of the study have been *misinterpreted*.
3 As the film was *subtitled*, it was accessible to many more audiences.
4 It was discovered that the problems were *interrelated*.
5 After the earthquake the building was *reconstructed*.
6 The computer needed to be replaced as the *microprocessor* was faulty.

> **STUDY SKILL** Composite words
>
> Some words are composed of identifiable parts: a prefix, a stem, and a suffix (see Study Skill p55), e.g. *unquestionably*
>
> prefix *un-*
> stem *question*
> suffix *-ably*
>
> Recognizing these parts can help you understand the meaning of these words.

READING SKILLS Dealing with longer texts (3) and (4)
LANGUAGE FOR SPEAKING Language for presentations
WRITING FOR SPEAKING How to be a good presenter • Preparing notes for a presentation • Giving a presentation
VOCABULARY DEVELOPMENT Formal and informal vocabulary

READING Communication technology

1 Work with a partner. Discuss the questions.
1 What methods of communication were used in the past?
2 What methods are used today?
3 What developments might there be in the future?

2 **Read Study Skill** Look at the title and headings of the text. Tick (✔) the topics you predict the text will contain.

a carrier pigeons   f radio
b computers   g telegraph
c flags (semaphore)   h telephones
d mirrors   i television
e newspapers   j typewriters

STUDY SKILL
Dealing with longer texts (3)

You do not always have to read all of a long text intensively. Decide which information you need. To do this:
- Predict what information the text will contain.
- Skim to check your predictions and to see how the information is organized.
- Select the parts of the text you need.

3 Skim the text. Were your predictions in exercise 2 right?

4 Skim the text again. Which paragraphs would you read intensively to get information about …
1 ☐ how the first telegraph system worked?
2 ☐ the early stages of computer technology?
3 ☐☐☐ the first three types of mobile phones?
4 ☐ future developments of mobile telephony?

Communication technology: a brief history
Transcript of a speech given by Dr Elizabeth Wallace

A The 21st century is already being described as the 'Information Age', not surprisingly, since communication and information technologies are widespread – in our homes, workplaces, and universities. It is probable that you have access to a mobile phone, radio, and television. It is equally likely that you have access to the global telecommunication network: the Internet. These forms of communication seem very modern, and yet the 'Information Age' of the early 21st century has a long and fascinating history.

The birth of electronic communication

B Deciding where to begin this history is difficult, but I would argue that our modern communication era started with the invention of telegraphy, literally, 'writing at a distance'. In 1830, scientist Joseph Henry used an electromagnet to force a steel bar to swing and ring a bell. This was the first electrical signalling.

C Samuel Morse developed this idea and invented the first practical telegraph in 1838. His system used an electrical circuit, a battery, a wire joining two telegraph stations, and an electromagnet. When a key was pressed onto the wire, it completed the electrical circuit, and then when it was released, it broke the circuit. This produced a clicking sound. For ease of communication, he developed the Morse code of dots and dashes.

D By the 1870s, news was travelling the world in seconds and many historic events such as the eruption of Krakatoa in 1883 and the sinking of the Titanic in 1912 were announced via the telegraph. However, despite this success, scientists and inventors were already considering how to transform the spoken word into electrical signals.

'Talking with electricity'

E Alexander Graham Bell understood the theory of a telephone, but struggled for a number of years to make a working model. Then, on March 10th 1876, he finally succeeded in transmitting speech. Bell's first telephone did not resemble the telephones of today, and over the next 100 years it underwent many changes. A microphone was added to produce a stronger signal. Then, the telephone 'bell' was attached, and users were given a unique 'telephone number'. Once amplifiers were added in the late 1920s, a telephone system was established that allowed people to talk across continents – the era of long-distance phone calls had arrived.

50 years of progress

F The first half of the 20th century saw enormous technical developments in three main areas: radio, television, and computers. Radio waves were the first to be explored, and in 1902, Marconi sent the first transatlantic radio signal. The first domestic radio with tuners to listen to different stations appeared only 14 years later, in 1916. Once radio was established, scientists and inventors started investigating the possibility of transmitting pictures. The leap from transmitting sound to broadcasting pictures took place in 1925, when John Logie Baird sent the first experimental television signal. By 1939, regular scheduled television broadcasting had begun.

G Computers were being developed at the same time as TV and radio, and in 1944, computers were put into public service for the first time. The first generation of modern programmed electronic computers were built in 1947 and used Random Access Memory (RAM). This is a 'memory' which allows access to any particular piece of information at almost any time. The smallest of these computers was the size of a family car and could store only about 8,000 words. Since they were so large and stored so little, computers had to change considerably to become as widespread as televisions and radios had.

Car-sized to pocket-sized computers

H From 1950 on, the development of computers was extremely rapid. In 1958, the integrated circuit or 'chip' was invented and computers started decreasing in size. In 1962, the first computer game, 'Spacewar', was sold, and computers became more popular. ARPANET, the original Internet, was launched in 1969, the first microprocessor was developed in 1971, and in 1981 the IBM PC (personal computer) was unveiled. The PC revolution had begun. Since then, computers have become smaller, faster, and 'smarter', and developed into what many of you use for your studies and entertainment today.

Mobile telephony: the first 25 years

I But how did these technical advances in radio, television, and computing affect telephonic communication? Perhaps surprisingly, it was the work on radio waves that was to have the biggest initial effect on the development of the telephone. The new era of phones worked by using radio waves which transmitted a radio signal to a transmission centre and then to the receiver. As they did not need to be attached to electrical wires, phones could be portable for the first time.

J The first generation (1G) phones were those developed in the 1980s. Much larger and heavier than today's mobile phones, these had a fairly limited range as the transmission networks were still being established.

K It was with the second generation (2G) phones, developed in the 90s, that the mobile truly entered the digital era. The new protocols of these phones, the rules that organize how devices connect to a network, were transmitted digitalized, and the Short Message Service (SMS) was added. Texting was born.

L The second and a half generation (2.5G) phones worked on the same network protocol as 2G phones, but added Wireless Application Protocol (WAP) and General Packet Radio Service (GPRS). These enabled mobile phones to access certain websites. In addition, some 2.5G phones had coloured screens and cameras.

M However, in 2000 a whole new generation of phones was launched: the third generation (3G). These were based on completely new protocols which enabled high-speed connections. A simple comparison illustrates this: the 2.5G phones on GPRS had an Internet access of 144b (bits) per second, whereas a 3G phone could be as fast as 2Mb (megabits) per second.

Multi-functions

N It is the fast connection that has allowed mobile phones to become multi-functional, and now many 3G phones are similar to Personal Digital Assistants (PDA), with operating systems (OS) such as Microsoft and Linux. These allow the phones to be used as mini-computers. Some have M-Commerce (Mobile Commerce) systems to allow the user to access, organize, and operate financial transactions such as making payments or selling stocks and shares. Many 3G phones also have the Global Positioning System (GPS), which enables users to know their exact position and to get directions to places they want to go.

O However, for many people it is the entertainment that mobiles provide that makes them so attractive. Users can play games, take pictures or make short films, listen to MP3 recordings, watch films, and tune into TV programmes in real time. The phones can also act as a modem, allowing owners to access their emails at any time.

What next?

P Research is already being carried out into Fourth Generation (4G) phones. These are expected to be launched in 2010. It is believed that the connection speed will rise to 100Mb per second. Other developments include the production of tiny wrist phones, holophones which project three-dimensional moving images of the owners, and remote-control of a car via your phone.

Q The development of the mobile phone has been rapid and astonishing. There is no real way of telling what developments are yet to come, but, as we have seen from this brief overview, communication technology has a long and exciting history. We cannot doubt that it has a long and exciting future, too.

(1242 words)

5 **Read Study Skill** Use the highlighted parts of the text to complete the notes below.

> **STUDY SKILL** Dealing with longer texts (4)
>
> To obtain the information from the selected text:
> - Read the selected parts of the text carefully. Highlight the information you need (see Study Skill p44).
> - Write headings and make numbered notes from the highlighted sections.
> - Check your notes. Is the information correct? Have you included all the important information?
> - Cover your notes and look at the headings. Recall the information you noted.

---

1 Origins of electronic communication
   1.1 Invention of telegraphy _____
   1.2 _____ 1838
   1.3 Historic examples of use
      1.3.i Krakatoa _____
      1.3.ii _____ _____

---

6 Find and correct three mistakes in the notes.

---

2 The telephone
   2.1 Speech first transmitted 1867
   2.2 Developments over 50 years
      2.2.i microphone added
      2.2.ii bell attached
      2.2.iii telephone book created
      2.2.iv amplifiers added
   2.3 First long-distance phone calls 1920s

---

7 Find the information on mobile phones in the text and complete the notes.

3 Mobile phones
   3.1 First generation (1G) 1980s
   3.2 _____ 1990s
      3.2.i digital transmission
      3.2.ii _____
   3.3 _____
      3.3.i WAP added
      3.3.ii _____
      3.3.iii access to websites
      3.3.iv _____ and _____
   3.4 _____
      3.4.i new protocols led to _____

---

8 Answer the questions without looking at the text or notes.

1 When were the 1G phones launched?
2 In what two ways were 2G phones different from 1G phones?
3 What could 2.5G phones do which 2G phones could not do?
4 When were 3G phones launched?
5 What was the effect of the new protocols on 3G phones?

LANGUAGE FOR SPEAKING Language for presentations

1 Write the phrases in the correct place in the table.

> To put it another way, …
> Next/Firstly/Secondly/Then/Finally I/we will look at/discuss …
> The first/second/next/last part …
> The subject of my talk/lecture/paper is …
> … that is to say, …
> My talk/lecture/paper is about …
>
> To conclude, …
> Let's turn our attention to …
> So, we have discussed …
> To summarize, …
> In conclusion, …
> Moving on, …

Introduction	I'm going to talk about …
Structure	This talk will be divided into … parts
Clarifying/rephrasing	In other words, …
Summarizing	To recap, …
Changing subject	Now, let's turn to …
Concluding	So, we have looked at …

2 Add a phrase from exercise 1 to the gaps.

> Good morning. ¹_____ the importance of English as an international
> language. ²_____ into four parts. ³_____ briefly
> describe the history of the English language. Secondly, I will describe the role of
> English today, especially in the fields of IT, science, technology, and medicine.
> ⁴_____ the role of English in popular culture,
> ⁵_____ music and films. ⁶_____ we will look at
> how we can ensure the continued success and development of our own language and
> culture at the same time as promoting the use of English as a tool of international
> communication.

3 Look at the prompt card for a presentation on *Computer Telephony*. Prepare the introduction to the presentation, using phrases and sentences from exercise 1.

> **1 Computer telephony**
>
> 1 Description
> 2 Benefits to users
> 3 Effects on land phone network providers
> 4 Effects on mobile phone network providers

4 Work with a partner. Give the introduction you prepared in exercise 3. Listen to your partner's introduction. Were they similar? Did you both use the phrases correctly? How could you improve your introduction or your partner's?

WRITING FOR SPEAKING Interpreting and translating

1 **Read Study Skill** Are the sentences part of written work (**W**), a spoken presentation (**S**), or both (**B**)?

> 1 Good morning everyone. **S**
> 2 I would like to talk about university education in Singapore.
> 3 This essay will explore the differences between dialects and accents.
> 4 Firstly, I shall describe the development of videoconferencing in the 1990s.
> 5 Let's turn our attention to why some countries do not teach a foreign language until secondary school.
> 6 As will become clear below, other languages are now becoming much more commonly used on the Internet.
> 7 Is everyone with me so far?
> 8 Therefore, to summarize, the main arguments in favour of early language education are as follows.
> 9 Are there any questions?
> 10 Let me put that another way.
> 11 In other words, English has become the main language of international trade and commerce.
> 12 Let me recap the main points so far.

STUDY SKILL
How to be a good presenter

An oral presentation can be more difficult to understand than a text. A good presenter should:

- introduce the subject and the structure of the talk at the beginning
- speak clearly
- explain, rephrase, and clarify new or difficult terms
- recap and summarize each section of the presentation.

2 **Read Study Skill** Look at the prompt card below and answer the questions.
   1 What is the title of the presentation?
   2 How many main sections are there?
   3 How many different types of interpreting will be discussed?

STUDY SKILL Preparing notes for a presentation

It is usually better to give a presentation from notes rather than reading aloud from a text.
- Make a card for each section of your talk and number the cards in the correct order.
- Give each card a main heading, e.g. *Title*, *Introduction*.
- Write notes using bullet points or numbers/letters (see Study Skill p61) to remind you of the main points.
- Write key phrases at the bottom of the card to either summarize that section of your presentation, or to move onto the next section, e.g. '*Let me recap the main points so far.*' or '*Now, let's turn to …*'.
- Practise your presentation at home. Time yourself and make sure it is the right length.

---

1 Interpreting
   1 Introduction – my name/topic – what is interpreting?/structure of presentation
   2 What qualifications are needed?
   3 Types of interpreting
      3.1 Simultaneous
      3.2 Consecutive
   4 Situations for interpreting
      4.1 Conferences
      4.2 Ad hoc
   5 Conclusion – addresses for further information

3 Prepare the introduction to the presentation, using phrases and sentences from exercise 1.

4 Read the paragraphs on how to become an interpreter and complete the notes on the prompt cards.

Minimum requirements

To become an interpreter, you will need a high standard of education. This could be a degree in interpreting, or a degree in languages with postgraduate training in interpreting. You must also have total mastery in your own language of the subject you wish to work in, e.g. sciences, technology.

You should have complete mastery of one foreign language, but more than one would be preferable. You must also have a thorough knowledge of that country's institutions, culture, attitudes, and practices.

You should also have a broad general knowledge, and be prepared to keep up to date with news and events around the world (in your foreign languages).

---

2 What qualifications are needed?

2.1 Education   i   degree in interpreting
               ii   degree in languages + _____

2.2 Languages   i   mastery of at least 1 foreign language
               ii   know _____

2.3 _____   i   broad
                       ii   _____

---

5 Read the paragraphs on interpreting and make notes on two prompt cards of your own.

Types of interpreting

Simultaneous interpreting
This is carried out from a booth, or small room, or by whispering the translation directly for one or two people. Simultaneous interpreters generally work from the foreign language into their mother tongue, i.e. a Spanish person would translate from the foreign language, say Arabic, into Spanish.

Consecutive interpreting
This occurs when the speaker (of the foreign language) pauses after each sentence or phrase to allow the interpreter to translate into the other language. Usually, the interpreter will need to take notes in order not to forget anything the speaker has said.

Situations for interpreting

Conference interpreting
This is a common situation for interpreting. It could be a national or international conference, a meeting, or an informal gathering. In fact, it could be anyplace where people who speak different languages gather together and need to communicate.

Ad-hoc interpreting
This is a service which is provided for people who are not fluent in a language of a country, but who need to communicate with the providers of services, such as the health, legal, and education services, in that language.

Giving a presentation

6 Choose a topic related to your studies or an essay you have written. Make notes on prompt cards to give a 5–10 minute presentation to your colleagues. Use words and phrases from *Language for Speaking* on page 79.

VOCABULARY DEVELOPMENT
Formal and informal vocabulary

1 **Read Study Skill** Choose the correct word or phrase in italics in sentences 1–6.

> **STUDY SKILL** Formal and informal vocabulary
>
> In academic and professional writing, use more formal vocabulary. For example:
> - single verbs, nouns, etc. rather than phrasal verbs and nouns, e.g. *increase* instead of *go up*
>
> If possible, avoid using words and phrases normally used in everyday spoken English.
> For example:
> *Lectures **commence** at **ten o'clock*** instead of *Lectures **begin** at **ten***.

1 The government *estimates/guesses* that prices will rise by 1% this year.
2 Phones today just don't *look like/resemble* phones from the 60s.
3 It is *a good idea/advisable* to arrive ten minutes before the examination begins.
4 The use of WiFi technology is now *widespread/ everywhere*.
5 Lots of young people *transmit/send* messages to their friends by SMS.
6 The mobile phone industry has announced that the cost of using mobile phones is expected to *decrease/go down* rapidly within the next two years.

2 Replace the underlined more informal words and phrases in the text with a more formal word or phrase from the box.

> are not able to   be very time-consuming   communicate   express
> represent   In the same way as   that is to say   As a result

Communicating without speaking

How can you ¹get your ideas <u>across</u> to people if you ²<u>can't</u> speak, perhaps because you are deaf? It would ³<u>take ages</u> to write down everything you needed to ⁴<u>say</u>. One solution is to use sign language. The recorded history of sign languages, ⁵<u>or to put it another way</u>, languages using one's hands, began in the sixteenth century. The gestures used by signers can ⁶<u>stand for</u> complete ideas in addition to single words. ⁷<u>Just like</u> spoken languages, signed languages vary from country to country and from region to region. ⁸<u>So</u>, there is a wide variety of sign languages in use around the world.

3 Look at the formal sentences and underline the more informal word or phrase.

1 For further information on courses in communication technology, get in touch with Dr Williams in the Department of Information Technology.
2 From 1950 to 2000, there were very big developments in the field of computer technology.
3 Please let the director know if there are any problems.
4 Students who miss classes as a result of illness are required to produce a medical certificate.
5 The director of the department will get here at 3pm.
6 All books must be brought back to the library by Monday 26th June.

4 Match a formal word or phrase with the informal words or phrases from exercise 3.

a are absent from **miss**   c contact _____   e returned _____
b arrive _____   d enormous _____   f inform _____

REVIEW

1 Read the text about WiFi technology and complete the notes.

WiFi technology

WiFi (wireless fidelity) refers to a local area network (LAN), which uses high frequency radio signals to send and receive data over short distances (about 60m).

The wireless network uses radio waves in a similar way to mobile phones and radios. The wireless adapter on a computer translates data into a radio signal and transmits it via an antenna. A wireless router receives the signal and decodes it. It then sends the data to the Internet.

The radio waves used for WiFi communication work at much higher frequencies than those used in other radio systems. This allows considerably more data to be transmitted. Also, WiFi radios can use three different frequency bands and can move between them. This means that there can be multiple devices using the same wireless connection simultaneously.

The number of WiFi networks is growing rapidly as they are easy and inexpensive to set up. Airports, shops, libraries, hotels, and even restaurants now provide these 'hotspots'. In addition, many cities are using the technology to provide free or low-cost Internet access for their residents.

Wireless networking is becoming so widespread that access to the Internet via cables and wires may soon be a thing of the past.

WiFi

1 **What is it?**
   1.1 Local area network (LAN)
   1.2 _____ radio signals
   1.3 _____ (60m)
2 **How does it work?**
   2.1 uses radio waves
   2.2 computer adapter translates data into _____
   2.3 radio signals transmitted _____
   2.4 _____ receives/decodes signal
   2.5 sent to the _____

3 **Advantages**
   3.1. more data can be sent
   3.2 _____ can use connection at the same time
4 **Developments**
   4.1 hotspots in _____
   4.2 cities can provide _____

2 Prepare a two-minute presentation on WiFi technology. Use phrases from *Language for Speaking* on page 79.

3 Go through the text on pages 76–77. What do the abbreviations stand for?

RAM **Random Access Memory**
PC   1G   SMS   WAP   3G
Mb   PDA   OS   GPS

4 Underline the phrasal verbs in the sentences. Replace each phrasal verb with a more formal verb from the box.

| accommodate | collect | complete | postponed | recovered from |

1 The new university hall can fit in 500 people.
2 Will all students pick up their essays from the secretary's office?
3 The director's meeting has been put off until next week.
4 We are pleased to announce that Dr Smith has got over his recent illness and will be returning to the university next week.
5 All new students must fill in their library membership forms by the end of this week.

WORDLIST

Here is a list of most of the
new words in the units of
New Headway Academic Skills
Level 3 Student's Book.

adj = adjective
adv = adverb
conj = conjunction
n = noun
pl = plural
prep = preposition
US = American English
v = verb

Unit 1

abbreviation *n* /əˌbriːviˈeɪʃn/
ability *n* /əˈbɪləti/
academic *adj* /ˌækəˈdemɪk/
accurate *adj* /ˈækjərət/
adjective *n* /ˈædʒɪktɪv/
agree *v* /əˈgriː/
alert *adj* /əˈlɜːt/
aloud *adj* /əˈlaʊd/
apply for *v* /əˈplaɪ fə/
approximately *adv* /əˈprɒksɪmətli/
article *n* /ˈɑːtɪkl/
assignment *n* /əˈsaɪnmənt/
attend *v* /əˈtend/
auditory *adj* /ˈɔːdɪtri/
auxiliary verb *n* /ɔːgˌzɪliəri ˈvɜːb/
available *adj* /əˈveɪləbl/
badge *n* /bædʒ/
basic *adj* /ˈbeɪsɪk/
biological *adj* /ˌbaɪəˈlɒdʒɪkl/
certainly *adv* /ˈsɜːtnli/
chart *n* /tʃɑːt/
check *v* /tʃek/
chemistry *n* /ˈkemɪstri/
choose *v* /tʃuːz/
co-educational *adj*
    /ˌkəʊedʒuˈkeɪʃənl/
collocate *v* /ˈkɒləkeɪt/
commitment *n* /kəˈmɪtmənt/
compare *v* /kəmˈpeə(r)/
complete *v* /kəmˈpliːt/
complicated *adj* /ˈkɒmplɪkeɪtɪd/
comprehensive *adj*
    /ˌkɒmprɪˈhensɪv/
compulsory *adj* /kəmˈpʌlsəri/
concentrate *v* /ˈkɒnsəntreɪt/
conclusion *n* /kənˈkluːʒn/
consist of *v* /kənˈsɪst əv/
content *n* /ˈkɒntent/
continue *v* /kənˈtɪnjuː/
contrast *v* /kənˈtrɑːst/
cram *v* /kræm/
crucial *adj* /ˈkruːʃl/
curriculum *n* /kəˈrɪkjələm/
daunting *adj* /ˈdɔːntɪŋ/

definite *adj* /ˈdefɪnət/
definition *n* /ˌdefɪˈnɪʃn/
delay *v* /dɪˈleɪ/
description *n* /dɪˈskrɪpʃn/
develop *v* /dɪˈveləp/
development *n* /dɪˈveləpmənt/
differ *v* /ˈdɪfə(r)/
difference *n* /ˈdɪfrəns/
discuss *v* /dɪˈskʌs/
discussion *n* /dɪˈskʌʃn/
divide *v* /dɪˈvaɪd/
draft *n* /drɑːft/
edition *n* /ɪˈdɪʃn/
education *n* /edʒuˈkeɪʃn/
effective *adj* /ɪˈfektɪv/
effectively *adv* /ɪˈfektɪvli/
encourage *v* /ɪnˈkʌrɪdʒ/
entrance exam *n* /ˈentrəns
    ɪgˌzæm/
essay *n* /ˈeseɪ/
expect *v* /ɪkˈspekt/
expression *n* /ɪkˈspreʃn/
extremely *adv* /ɪkˈstriːmli/
find out *v* /ˌfaɪnd ˈaʊt/
form *n* /fɔːm/
formula *n* /ˈfɔːmjələ/
full-time *adj* /ˌfʊlˈtaɪm/
further *adv* /ˈfɜːðə(r)/
generally *adv* /ˈdʒenrəli/
grammar *n* /ˈgræmə(r)/
graph *n* /grɑːf/
habit *n* /ˈhæbɪt/
hand in *v* /ˌhænd ˈɪn/
hardly ever *adv* /ˌhɑːdli ˈevə/
heading *n* /ˈhedɪŋ/
hold *v* /həʊld/
however *adv* /haʊˈevə(r)/
illustration *n* /ˌɪləˈstreɪʃn/
immediately *adv* /ɪˈmiːdiətli/
improve *v* /ɪmˈpruːv/
incentive *n* /ɪnˈsentɪv/
include *v* /ɪnˈkluːd/
inorganic *adj* /ˌɪnɔːˈgænɪk/
intensive *adj* /ɪnˈtensɪv/
intransitive *adj* /ɪnˈtrænsətɪv/
irregular *adj* /ɪˈregjələ(r)/
journal *n* /ˈdʒɜːnl/
law *n* /lɔː/
lecture *n* /ˈlektʃə(r)/
lecturer *n* /ˈlektʃərə(r)/
linking word *n* /ˈlɪŋkɪŋ ˌwɜːd/
list *n* /lɪst/
literature *n* /ˈlɪtrətʃə(r)/
locate *v* /ləʊˈkeɪt/
main *n* /meɪn/
majority *n* /məˈdʒɒrəti/
manageable *adj* /ˈmænɪdʒəbl/
management *n* /ˈmænɪdʒmənt/
match *v* /mætʃ/
material *n* /məˈtɪəriəl/
meaning *n* /ˈmiːnɪŋ/
memorize *v* /ˈmeməraɪz/

mention *v* /ˈmenʃn/
mixture *n* /ˈmɪkstʃə(r)/
module *n* /ˈmɒdjuːl/
national *adj* /ˈnæʃnəl/
neat *adj* /niːt/
necessary *v* /ˈnesəsəri/
note *n* /nəʊt/
occur *v* /əˈkɜː(r)/
on the other hand /ˌɒn ðə ˈʌðə
    hænd/
organic *adj* /ɔːˈgænɪk/
organize *v* /ˈɔːgənaɪz/
overseas *adj* /ˌəʊvəˈsiːz/
overview *n* /ˈəʊvəvjuː/
part of speech *n* /ˌpɑːt əv ˈspiːtʃ/
participle *n* /pɑːˈtɪsɪpl/
particular *n* /pəˈtɪkjələ(r)/
phrase *n* /freɪz/
physical education *n* /ˌfɪzɪkl
    edʒuˈkeɪʃn/
plan *n, v* /plæn/
plural *n* /ˈplʊərəl/
poem *n* /ˈpəʊɪm/
preposition *n* /ˌprepəˈzɪʃn/
previous *adj* /ˈpriːviəs/
private *adj* /ˈpraɪvət/
problem *n* /ˈprɒbləm/
process *n* /ˈprəʊses/
pronunciation *n* /prəˌnʌnsiˈeɪʃn/
punctuation *n* /ˌpʌŋktjuˈeɪʃn/
put off *v* /ˌpʊt ˈɒf/
qualifications *n pl*
    /ˌkwɒlɪfɪˈkeɪʃnz/
quality *n* /ˈkwɒləti/
quotation *n* /kwəʊˈteɪʃn/
realistic *adj* /ˌriːəˈlɪstɪk/
reason *n* /ˈriːzn/
receive *v* /rɪˈsiːv/
recent *adj* /ˈriːsnt/
record *v* /rɪˈkɔːd/
refer to *v* /rɪˈfɜː tu/
register *v* /ˈredʒɪstə(r)/
relevant *adj* /ˈreləvənt/
remain *v* /rɪˈmeɪn/
require *v* /rɪˈkwaɪə(r)/
research *v* /rɪˈsɜːtʃ/
research *n* /rɪˈsɜːtʃ/
result *n* /rɪˈzʌlt/
retrieve *v* /rɪˈtriːv/
revise *v* /rɪˈvaɪz/
revision *n* /rɪˈvɪʒn/
reward *n* /rɪˈwɔːd/
score *n* /skɔː(r)/
secondary *adj* /ˈsekəndri/
serious *adj* /ˈsɪəriəs/
set *v* /set/
several *pron* /ˈsevrəl/
significant *adj* /sɪgˈnɪfɪkənt/
similar *adj* /ˈsɪmələ(r)/
similarity *n* /ˌsɪməˈlærəti/
sit *v* /sɪt/
skill *n* /skɪl/

skim *v* /skɪm/
society *n* /səˈsaɪəti/
source *n* /sɔːs/
specialize *v* /ˈspeʃəlaɪz/
specific *adj* /spəˈsɪfɪk/
spelling *n* /ˈspelɪŋ/
staff *n* /stɑːf/
state *adj* /steɪt/
stress *n* /stres/
style *n* /staɪl/
subject *n* /ˈsʌbdʒɪkt/
suit *v* /suːt/
survey *v* /səˈveɪ/
syllable *n* /ˈsɪləbl/
symbol *n* /ˈsɪmbl/
system *n* /ˈsɪstəm/
table *n* /ˈteɪbl/
target *n* /ˈtɑːgɪt/
tense *n* /tens/
term *n* /tɜːm/
tertiary *adj* /ˈtɜːʃəri/
text *n* /tekst/
timing *n* /ˈtaɪmɪŋ/
title *n* /ˈtaɪtl/
topic *n* /ˈtɒpɪk/
transitive *adj* /ˈtrænsətɪv/
tutor *n* /ˈtjuːtə(r)/
underline *v* /ˌʌndəˈlaɪn/
usually *adv* /ˈjuːʒəli/
vague *adj* /veɪg/
vast *adj* /vɑːst/
visual *adj* /ˈvɪʒuəl/
vocabulary *n* /vəˈkæbjələri/
well-organized *adj*
    /ˌwelˈɔːgənaɪzd/
whereas *conj* /ˌweərˈæz/
whether *conj* /ˈweðə(r)/
worthwhile *adj* /ˌwɜːθˈwaɪl/

Unit 2

accelerate *v* /əkˈseləreɪt/
accept *v* /əkˈsept/
according to /əˈkɔːdɪŋ tə/
action *n* /ˈækʃn/
activate *v* /ˈæktɪveɪt/
adult *n* /ˈædʌlt/
advanced *adj* /ədˈvɑːnst/
affected by *v* /əˈfektɪd baɪ/
alternative *n* /ɔːlˈtɜːnətɪv/
amount *n* /əˈmaʊnt/
ancient *adj* /ˈeɪnʃnt/
anecdotal *adj* /ˌænɪkˈdəʊtl/
antibiotics *n pl* /ˌæntibaɪˈɒtɪks/
approach *v* /əˈprəʊtʃ/
associate with *v* /əˈsəʊʃieɪt wɪð/
attack *v* /əˈtæk/
attribute *v* /æˈtrɪbjuːt/
balance *v* /ˈbæləns/
balanced *adj* /ˈbælənst/
base on *v* /ˈbeɪs ɒn/
beneficial *adj* /ˌbenɪˈfɪʃl/
benefit *n* /ˈbenɪfɪt/
body *n* /ˈbɒdi/
brain *n* /breɪn/
brainstorm *v* /ˈbreɪnstɔːm/
cancel *v* /ˈkænsl/
cancer *n* /ˈkænsə(r)/
carry out *v* /ˌkæri ˈaʊt/
cause *n* /kɔːz/
cell *n* /sel/
century *n* /ˈsentʃəri/
change *n, v* /tʃeɪndʒ/
common *adj* /ˈkɒmən/
completely *adv* /kəmˈpliːtli/
concern *n* /kənˈsɜːn/
conclude *v* /kənˈkluːd/
condition *n* /kənˈdɪʃn/
conduct *v* /kənˈdʌkt/
confirm *v* /kənˈfɜːm/
confusion *n* /kənˈfjuːʒn/
connection *n* /kəˈnekʃn/
consider *v* /kənˈsɪdə(r)/
constantly *adv* /ˈkɒnstəntli/
consumption *n* /kənˈsʌmpʃn/
copy *v* /ˈkɒpi/
correct *adj* /kəˈrekt/
credit *v* /ˈkredɪt/
cure *n, v* /kjʊə(r)/
currently *adv* /ˈkʌrəntli/
curriculum *n* /kəˈrɪkjələm/
cut *v* /kʌt/
daily *adv* /ˈdeɪli/
damage *n, v* /ˈdæmɪdʒ/
data *n* /ˈdeɪtə/
demand *v* /dɪˈmɑːnd/
depend on *v* /dɪˈpend ɒn/
destroy *v* /dɪˈstrɔɪ/
detail *n* /ˈdiːteɪl/
develop *v* /dɪˈveləp/
diet *n* /ˈdaɪət/
directly *adv* /dəˈrektli/
disability *n* /ˌdɪsəˈbɪləti/
disease *n* /dɪˈziːz/
divide *v* /dɪˈvaɪd/
document *n, v* /ˈdɒkjəmənt/
due to *adj* /ˈdjuː tə/

effect *n* /ɪˈfekt/
effective *adj* /ɪˈfektɪv/
electrical *adj* /ɪˈlektrɪkl/
encouraging *adj* /ɪnˈkʌrɪdʒɪŋ/
essential *adj* /ɪˈsenʃl/
evidence *n* /ˈevɪdəns/
exercise *n* /ˈeksəsaɪz/
explain *v* /ɪkspleɪn/
fact *n* /fækt/
fewer *adj* /ˈfjuːə(r)/
finding *n* /ˈfaɪndɪŋ/
focus *n, v* /ˈfəʊkəs/
general *adj* /ˈdʒenrl/
growth *n* /grəʊθ/
guideline *n* /ˈgaɪdlaɪn/
harmful *adj* /ˈhɑːmfl/
heal *v* /hiːl/
health *n* /helθ/
illness *n* /ˈɪlnəs/
immune system *n* /ɪmˈjuːn ˌsɪstəm/
important *adj* /ɪmˈpɔːtənt/
in fact /ɪn ˈfækt/
include *v* /ɪnˈkluːd/
increase *v* /ɪnˈkriːs/
ineffective *adj* /ˌɪnɪˈfektɪv/
inject *v* /ɪnˈdʒekt/
innovation *n* /ˌɪnəˈveɪʃn/
investigate *v* /ɪnˈvestɪgeɪt/
involved in *v* /ɪnˈvɒlvd ɪn/
kill *v* /kɪl/
laboratory *n* /ləˈbɒrətri/
lack of *n* /ˈlæk əv/
lead *v* /liːd/
level *n* /ˈlevl/
lifestyle *n* /ˈlaɪfstaɪl/
limb *n* /lɪm/
limit *n* /ˈlɪmɪt/
long-term *adj* /ˌlɒŋˈtɜːm/
loss *n* /lɒs/
lower *adj* /ˈləʊə(r)/
maintain *v* /meɪnˈteɪn/
manufacture *v* /ˌmænjuˈfæktʃə/
medical *adj* /ˈmedɪkl/
medical condition *n* /ˈmedɪkl kənˌdɪʃn/
message *n* /ˈmesɪdʒ/
mixture *n* /ˈmɪkstʃə/
monitor *v* /ˈmɒnɪtə(r)/
mysterious *adj* /mɪˈstɪəriəs/
need *v* /niːd/
observation *n* /ˌɒbzəˈveɪʃn/
obvious *adj* /ˈɒbviəs/
opinion *n* /əˈpɪnjən/
overuse *v* /ˌəʊvəˈjuːz/
paraphrase *v* /ˈpærəfreɪz/
participate *v* /pɑːˈtɪsɪpeɪt/
patient *n* /ˈpeɪʃnt/
performance *n* /pəˈfɔːməns/
physical *adj* /ˈfɪzɪkl/
plagiarism *n* /ˈpleɪdʒərɪzəm/
population *n* /ˌpɒpjuˈleɪʃn/
portion *n* /ˈpɔːʃn/
positive *adj* /ˈpɒzətɪv/
practitioner *n* /prækˈtɪʃənə(r)/
predict *v* /prɪˈdɪkt/
prescribe *v* /prɪˈskraɪb/
pretend *v* /prɪˈtend/

previously *adv* /ˈpriːviəsli/
process *n* /ˈprəʊses/
profession *n* /prəˈfeʃn/
progress *n* /ˈprəʊgres/
promising *adj* /ˈprɒmɪsɪŋ/
proof *n* /pruːf/
protect *v* /prəˈtekt/
provide *v* /prəˈvaɪd/
publish *v* /ˈpʌblɪʃ/
radiation *n* /ˌreɪdiˈeɪʃn/
recommend *v* /ˌrekəˈmend/
recover *v* /rɪˈkʌvə(r)/
recovery *n* /rɪˈkʌvəri/
rediscovery *n* /ˌriːdɪˈskʌvəri/
reduce *v* /rɪˈdjuːs/
relate to *v* /rɪˈleɪt tə/
remember *v* /rɪˈmembə(r)/
rephrase *v* /ˌriːˈfreɪz/
replace *v* /rɪˈpleɪs/
report *v* /rɪˈpɔːt/
require *v* /rɪˈkwaɪə(r)/
researcher *n* /rɪˈsɜːtʃə(r)/
rest *v* /rest/
result *n* /rɪˈzʌlt/
rhythm *n* /ˈrɪðəm/
risk *n* /rɪsk/
scientist *n* /ˈsaɪəntɪst/
sensible *adj* /ˈsensəbl/
show *v* /ʃəʊ/
sight *n* /saɪt/
signal *n* /ˈsɪgnəl/
sound *n* /saʊnd/
specialist *n* /ˈspeʃəlɪst/
specifically *adv* /spəˈsɪfɪkli/
speed *n* /spiːd/
spread *v* /spred/
stage *n* /steɪdʒ/
stimulate *v* /ˈstɪmjuleɪt/
stress *n* /ˈstres/
structure *n* /ˈstrʌktʃə(r)/
study *n* /ˈstʌdi/
subject *n* /ˈsʌbdʒɪkt/
substance *n* /ˈsʌbstəns/
suffer from *v* /ˈsʌfə frəm/
suggest *v* /səˈdʒest/
suitable *adj* /ˈsuːtəbl/
summarize *v* /ˈsʌməraɪz/
summary *n* /ˈsʌməri/
synonym *n* /ˈsɪnənɪm/
target *v, n* /ˈtɑːgɪt/
test *v, n* /test/
theory *n* /ˈθɪəri/
therapy *n* /ˈθerəpi/
treat *v* /triːt/
treatment *n* /ˈtriːtmənt/
trial *n* /ˈtraɪəl/
truth *n* /truːθ/
unhealthy *adj* /ʌnˈhelθi/
vaccine *n* /ˈvæksiːn/
various *adj* /ˈveəriəs/
weight *n* /weɪt/
well-being *n* /ˈwelbiːɪŋ/
well-developed *adj* /ˌweldɪˈveləpt/
wound *n* /wuːnd/

Unit 3

accommodation *n*
/ə,kɒmə'deɪʃn/
add *v* /æd/
address *v* /ə'dres/
administrative *adj*
/əd'mɪnɪstrətɪv/
advantages *n pl* /əd'va:ntɪdʒɪz/
advisor *n* /əd'vaɪzə(r)/
agriculture *n* /'ægrɪkʌltʃə(r)/
apparent *adj* /ə'pærənt/
appear *v* /ə'pɪə(r)/
appoint *v* /ə'pɔɪnt/
architect *n* /'ɑ:kɪtekt/
argue *v* /'ɑ:gju:/
arguments *n pl* /'ɑ:gjumənts/
as stated in *v* /æz 'steɪtɪd ɪn/
aspects *n pl* /'æspekts/
atmosphere *n* /'ætməsfɪə(r)/
attempt *v* /ə'tempt/
availability *n* /ə,veɪlə'bɪləti/
average *adj* /'ævərɪdʒ/
backward *prep* /'bækwəd/
base in *v* /'beɪs ɪn/
boat *n* /bəʊt/
borders *n pl* /'bɔ:dəz/
bridges *n pl* /'brɪdʒɪz/
building *n* /'bɪldɪŋ/
business park *n* /'bɪznəs pɑ:k/
capital *n* /'kæpɪtl/
challenge *n* /'tʃæləndʒ/
choice *n* /tʃɔɪs/
climate *n* /'klaɪmət/
coast *n* /kəʊst/
coastal *adj* /'kəʊstl/
cohesion *n* /kəʊ'hi:ʒn/
colleagues *n pl* /'kɒli:gz/
collocate *v* /'kɒləkeɪt/
collocation *n* /,kɒlə'keɪʃn/
commence *v* /kə'mens/
commerce *n* /'kɒmɜ:s/
commercial *adj* /kə'mɜ:ʃl/
commission *n* /kə'mɪʃn/
committee *n* /kə'mɪti/
community *n* /kə'mju:nəti/
compete *v* /kəm'pi:t/
complete *v* /kəm'pli:t/
conclude *v* /kən'klu:d/
conference *n* /'kɒnfrəns/
consequences *n pl*
/'kɒnsɪkwənsɪz/
consequently *adv*
/'kɒnsɪkwəntli/
consideration *n* /kən,sɪdə'reɪʃn/
construction *n* /kən'strʌkʃn/
continually *adv* /kɒn'tɪnjuəli/
continuity *n* /,kɒntɪ'nju:əti/
courageous *adj* /kə'reɪdʒəs/
create *v* /kri:'eɪt/
cross *v* /krɒs/
cross out *v* /,krɒs 'aʊt/
cultural *adj* /'kʌltʃərəl/
deal with *v* /'di:l wɪð/
demand *n* /dɪ'mɑ:nd/
demonstrate *v* /'demənstreɪt/
depend on *v* /dɪ'pend ɒn/
describe *v* /dɪ'skraɪb/

developments *n pl*
/dɪ'veləpmənts/
diploma *n* /dɪ'pləʊmə/
disadvantages *n pl*
/,dɪsəd'va:ntɪdʒɪz/
discursive essay *n* /dɪ,skɜ:rsɪv
'eseɪ/
discuss *v* /dɪ'skʌs/
district *n* /'dɪstrɪkt/
divide *v* /dɪ'vaɪd/
draw up *v* /,drɔ: 'ʌp/
drawbacks *n pl* /'drɔ:bæks/
economic *adj* /,i:kə'nɒmɪk/
employ *v* /ɪm'plɔɪ/
environment *n* /ɪn'vaɪrənmənt/
error *n* /'erə(r)/
establish *v* /ɪ'stæblɪʃ/
evaluate *v* /ɪ'væljueɪt/
event *n* /ɪ'vent/
example *n* /ɪg'za:mpl/
existing *adj* /ɪg'zɪstɪŋ/
experience *n* /ɪk'spɪəriəns/
experiment *n, v* /ɪk'sperɪmənt/
face *v* /feɪs/
facilities *n pl* /fə'sɪləti:z/
factors *n pl* /'fæktəz/
factual *adj* /'fæktʃuəl/
farming *n* /'fɑ:mɪŋ/
final *adj* /faɪnl/
finally *adv* /'faɪnəli/
first-class *adj* /,fɜ:st 'klɑ:s/
flow *v* /fləʊ/
for this reason /fə ,ðɪs 'ri:zn/
forward *prep* /'fɔ:wəd/
found *v* /faʊnd/
frequently *adv* /'fri:kwəntli/
functions *n pl* /'fʌŋkʃnz/
furthermore *adv*
/,fɜ:ðə'mɔ:(r)/
growth *n* /grəʊθ/
heavily *adv* /'hevɪli/
historic *adj* /hɪ'stɒrɪk/
hospital *n* /'hɒspɪtl/
household *n* /'haʊshəʊld/
housing *n* /'haʊzɪŋ/
identify *v* /aɪ'dentɪfaɪ/
immigrants *n pl* /'ɪmɪgrənts/
importance *n* /ɪm'pɔ:təns
industry *n* /'ɪndəstri/
influence *n* /'ɪnfluəns/
inhabitants *n pl* /ɪn'hæbɪtənts/
initial *adj* /ɪ'nɪʃl/
innovative *adj* /'ɪnəvətɪv/
instructions *n pl* /ɪn'strʌkʃnz/
integrate *v* /'ɪntɪgreɪt/
introduction *n* /,ɪntrə'dʌkʃn/
investigate *v* /ɪn'vestɪgeɪt/
jumbled *adj* /'dʒʌmbld/
leader *n* /'li:də(r)/
locations *n pl* /ləʊ'keɪʃnz/
logical *adj* /'lɒdʒɪkl/
low level *adj* /,ləʊ 'levl/
minimize *v* /'mɪnɪmaɪz/
model *n* /'mɒdl/
modern *adj* /'mɒdn/
mountain range *n* /'maʊntən
,reɪndʒ/
national *adj* /'næʃnəl/

natural *adj* /'nætʃrəl/
network *n* /'netwɜ:k/
options *n pl* /'ɒpʃnz/
order *n* /'ɔ:də(r)/
original *adj* /ə'rɪgənl/
overall *adj* /,əʊvə'rɔ:l/
overcome *v* /,əʊvə'kʌm/
overcrowding *n* /,əʊvə'kraʊdɪŋ/
persuade *v* /pə'sweɪd/
persuasive *adj* /pə'sweɪsɪv/
phrases *n pl* /'freɪzɪz/
physicist *n* /'fɪzɪsɪst/
pollution *n* /pə'lu:ʃn/
possible *adj* /'pɒsəbl/
preserve *v* /prɪ'zɜ:v/
pressure *n* /'preʃə(r)/
prioritise *v* /praɪ'ɒrətaɪz/
priority *n* /praɪ'ɒrəti/
private *adj* /'praɪvət/
problems *n pl* /'prɒbləmz/
produce *v* /prə'dju:s/
properly *adv* /'prɒpəli/
proposal *n* /prə'pəʊzl/
public *n* /'pʌblɪk/
purpose *n* /'pɜ:pəs/
quotation marks *n pl* /kwəʊ'teɪʃn
,ma:ks/
rapidly *adv* /'ræpɪdli/
realize *v* /'ri:əlaɪz/
recreation *n* /,rekri'eɪʃn/
recycling *n* /,ri:'saɪklɪŋ/
re-development *n*
/,ri:dɪ'veləpmənt/
reference *n* /'refrəns/
reference material *n* /'refrəns
mə,tɪəriəl/
regional *adj* /'ri:dʒənl/
religious *adj* /rɪ'lɪdʒəs/
rethink *v* /,ri:'θɪŋk/
review *v* /rɪv'ju:/
roads *n pl* /rəʊdz/
role *n* /rəʊl/
rubbish *n* /'rʌbɪʃ/
sanitation *n* /,sænɪ'teɪʃn/
scheme *n* /ski:m/
search *v* /sɜ:tʃ/
section *n* /'sekʃn/
select *v* /sɪ'lekt/
seminar *n* /'semɪna:(r)/
sensible *adj* /'sensəbl/
separately *adv* /'seprətli/
services *n pl* /'sɜ:vɪsɪs/
site *n* /saɪt/
social *adj* /'səʊʃl/
solution *n* /sə'lu:ʃn/
space *n* /speɪs/
split *v* /splɪt/
superb *adj* /su:'pɜ:b/
supplies *n pl* /sə'plaɪz/
thriving *adj* /'θraɪvɪŋ/
throughout *prep* /θru:'aʊt/
together *adv* /tə'geðə(r)/
top-quality *adj* /,tɒp 'kwɒlɪti/
trade fair *n* /'treɪd ,feə(r)/
traffic congestion *n* /'træfɪk
kən,dʒestʃn/
transport *n* /'trænspɔ:t/
transportation *n* /,trænspɔ:'teɪʃn/

unfortunately *adv* /ʌn'fɔ:tʃənətli/
urban planning *n* /'ɜ:bn ,plænɪŋ/
various *adj* /'veəriəs/
waste *n* /weɪst/
well-written *adj* /,wel'rɪtn/

Unit 4

abundant *adj* /ə'bʌndənt/
act as *v* /'ækt əz/
adequate *adj* /'ædɪkwət/
annually *adv* /'ænjuəli/
Antarctic *n* /æn'tɑːktɪk/
apartment blocks *n pl*
   /ə'pɑːtmənt ˌblɒks/
as a result /ˌæz ə rɪ'zʌlt/
billion *n* /'bɪljən/
both *pron* /bəʊθ/
break down *v* /ˌbreɪk 'daʊn/
briefcase *n* /'briːfkeɪs/
build *v* /bɪld/
carbon dioxide *n* /ˌkɑːbən
   daɪ'ɒksaɪd/
centuries *n pl* /'sentʃəriz/
chain *n* /tʃeɪn/
characteristic *n* /ˌkærəktə'rɪstɪk/
classified *adj* /'klæsɪfaɪd/
collect *v* /kə'lekt/
combination *n* /ˌkɒmbɪn'eɪʃn/
combine *v* /kəm'baɪn/
compensate *v* /'kɒmpənseɪt/
competition *n* /ˌkɒm'pətɪʃn/
compound *n* /'kɒmpaʊnd/
concern *n* /kən'sɜːn/
conditions *n pl* /kən'dɪʃnz/
consequently *adv* /'kɒnsɪkwəntli/
conserve *v* /kən'sɜːv/
considerably *adv* /kən'sɪdrəbli/
construct *v* /kəns'trʌkt/
consumer *n* /kən'sjuːmə(r)/
contaminants *n pl*
   /kən'tæmɪnənts/
convert *v* /kən'vɜːt/
cost *n* /kɒst/
crude oil *n* /ˌkruːd 'ɔɪl/
dependent on *adj* /dɪ'pendənt
   ɒn/
desalination *n* /ˌdiːˌsælɪn'eɪʃn/
die *v* /daɪ/
directly *adv* /də'rektli/
earth *n* /ɜːθ/
economically *adv* /ˌiːkə'nɒmɪkli/
efficiency *n* /ɪ'fɪʃnsi/
end *v, n* /end/
energy *n* /'enədʒi/
eventually *adv* /ɪ'ventʃuəli/
everywhere *adv* /'evriweə(r)/
examine *v* /ɪg'zæmɪn/
expect *v* /ɪk'spekt/
expensive *adj* /ɪk'spensɪv/
explain *v* /ɪk'spleɪn/
exploit *v* /ɪk'splɔɪt/
express *v* /ɪk'spres/
factory *n* /'fæktri/
farm *n* /fɑːm/
feed *v* /fiːd/
for instance /fər 'ɪnstəns/
form *v* /fɔːm/
fossil fuels *n pl* /'fɒsl fjuːəlz/
functions *n pl* /'fʌŋkʃnz/
generally *adv* /'dʒenrəli/
generate *v* /'dʒenəreɪt/
global warming *n* /ˌgləʊbl
   'wɔːmɪŋ/

governments *n pl* /'gʌvənmənts/
guideline *n* /'gaɪdlaɪn/
heartbeat *n* /'hɑːtbiːt/
heating *n, adj* /'hiːtɪŋ/
hope *v* /həʊp/
hyphenated *adj* /'haɪfəneɪtɪd/
in brief /ɪn 'briːf/
in conclusion /ˌɪn kən'kluːʒn/
in use *adj* /ˌɪn 'juːs/
indicate *v* /'ɪndɪkeɪt/
industrial *adj* /ɪn'dʌstriəl/
inexpensive *adj* /ˌɪnɪk'spensɪv/
install *v* /ɪn'stɔːl/
lab coat *n* /'læb ˌkəʊt/
leaves *n pl* /liːvz/
manage *v* /'mænɪdʒ/
maximize *v* /'mæksɪmaɪz/
medicine *n* /'medsn/
medium *adj* /'miːdiəm/
micro *adj* /'maɪkrəʊ/
mineral water *n* /'mɪnərəl
   ˌwɔːtə(r)/
molecules *n pl* /'mɒlɪkjuːlz/
movement *n* /'muːvmənt/
obliged *adj* /ə'blaɪdʒd/
official *adj* /ə'fɪʃl/
oil refining *n* /'ɔɪl rɪˌfaɪnɪŋ/
operate *v* /'ɒpəreɪt/
organism *n* /'ɔːgənɪzəm/
outline *n* /'aʊtlaɪn/
oxygen *n* /'ɒksɪdʒən/
paper *n* /'peɪpə(r)/
participation *n* /pɑːˌtɪsɪ'peɪʃn/
parts *n pl* /pɑːts/
petrol *n* /'petrəl/
pipe *n* /paɪp/
precious *adj* /'preʃəs/
products *n pl* /'prɒdʌkts/
propose *v* /prə'pəʊz/
prove *v* /pruːv/
public *n* /'pʌblɪk/
purify *v* /'pjʊərɪfaɪ/
rapid *adj* /'ræpɪd/
raw materials *n pl* /ˌrɔː
   mə'tɪəriəlz/
regularly *adv* /'regjələli/
relationship *n* /rɪ'leɪʃnʃɪp/
relatively *adv* /'relətɪvli/
release *v* /rɪ'liːs/
removal *n* /rɪ'muːvl/
remove *v* /rɪ'muːv/
renewable *adj* /rɪ'njuːəbl/
repair *v* /rɪ'peə(r)/
reproduction *n* /ˌriːprə'dʌkʃn/
reservoir *n* /'rezəvwɑː(r)/
resource *n* /rɪ'zɔːs/
respiration *n* /ˌrespə'reɪʃn/
review *n, v* /rɪv'juː/
rise *v* /raɪz/
roots *n pl* /ruːts/
rules *n pl* /ruːlz/
secondary *adj* /'sekəndri/
sequence *n* /'siːkwəns/
serious *adj* /'sɪəriəs/
shortage *n* /'ʃɔːtɪdʒ/
skyscraper *n* /'skaɪskreɪpə(r)/
steps *n pl* /steps/
subsequent *adj* /'sʌbsɪkwənt/

succeed *v* /sək'siːd/
successful *adj* /sək'sesfl/
sum up *v* /ˌsʌm 'ʌp/
supply *n* /sə'plaɪ/
surface *n* /'sɜːfɪs/
take for granted *v* /ˌteɪk fə
   'grɑːntɪd/
tap *n* /tæp/
technology *n* /tek'nɒlədʒi/
tips *n pl* /tɪps/
traditionally *adv* /trə'dɪʃənəli/
transfer *v* /træns'fɜː(r)/
turn into *v* /ˌtɜːn ɪntuː/
turn to *v* /'tɜːn tu/
undrinkable *adj* /ʌn'drɪŋkəbl/
unique *adj* /juː'niːk/
utilize *v* /'juːtəlaɪz/
valuable *adj* /'væljuəbl/
whales *n pl* /'weɪlz/
widespread *adj* /'waɪdspred/
wood *n* /wʊd/

Unit 5

abroad *adj* /əˈbrɔːd/
accountancy *n* /əˈkaʊntənsi/
accumulate *v* /əˈkjuːmjəleɪt/
acquire *v* /əˈkwaɪə(r)/
adverse *adj* /ˈædvɜːs/
afford *v* /əˈfɔːd/
against *adj* /əˈɡenst/
agreement *n* /əˈɡriːmənt/
analyse *v* /ˈænəlaɪz/
anti-globalists *n pl*
   /ˌæntɪˈɡləʊbəlɪsts/
appear *adv* /əˈpɪə(r)/
arguments *n pl* /ˈɑːɡjumənts/
as a result /ˌæz ə ˈrɪzʌlt/
as far as I am concerned /æz ˌfɑːr
   əz ˈaɪm kənˌsɜːnd/
astronomer *n* /əˈstrɒnəmə(r)/
at present /ət ˈpreznt/
aware *v* /əˈweə(r)/
balanced *adj* /ˈbælənst/
believe *v* /ˈbɪliːv/
calculate *v* /ˈkælkjuleɪt/
caution *n* /ˈkɔːʃn/
certainty *n* /ˈsɜːtənti/
charge *v* /ˈtʃɑːdʒ/
chemicals *n pl* /ˈkemɪklz/
cite *v* /saɪt/
claim *v* /kleɪm/
commercial *adj* /kəˈmɜːʃl/
commodities *n pl* /kəˈmɒdətiz/
concerns *n pl* /kənˈsɜːnz/
consumerism *n* /kənˈsuːmərɪzəm/
consumers *n pl* /kənˈsuːməz/
consumption *n* /kənˈsʌmpʃn/
contract *v* /kənˈtrækt/
contract *n* /ˈkɒntrækt/
control *n, v* /kənˈtrəʊl/
critical *adj* /ˈkrɪtɪkl/
critically *adv* /ˈkrɪtɪkli/
damage *v, n* /ˈdæmɪdʒ/
debate *v* /dɪˈbeɪt/
debts *n pl* /dets/
decide *v* /dɪˈsaɪd/
decrease *v* /dɪˈkriːs/
define *v* /dɪˈfaɪn/
degree *n* /dɪˈɡriː/
desire *n* /dɪˈzaɪə(r)/
despite the fact that /dɪˈspaɪt ðə
   ˌfækt ðət/
destination *n* /ˌdestɪˈneɪʃn/
direct *adj* /dəˈrekt/
dispose of *v* /dɪˈspəʊz əv/
distinguishing *adj* /dɪˈstɪŋɡwɪʃɪŋ/
doubt *v* /daʊt/
drastically *adv* /ˈdræstɪkli/
earn *v* /ɜːn/
earthquake *n* /ˈɜːθkweɪk/
economic powers *n pl*
   /ˈiːkənɒmɪk ˌpaʊəz/
economy *n* /ɪˈkɒnəmi/
enormously *adv* /ɪˈnɔːməsli/
environmental *adj*
   /ɪnˌvaɪrənˈmentl/
equally *adv* /ˈiːkwəli/
equipment *n* /ɪˈkwɪpmənt/
ethical *adj* /ˈeθɪkl/

evaluate *v* /ɪˈvæljueɪt/
examiner *n* /ɪɡˈzæmɪnə(r)/
exchange *v* /ɪksˈtʃeɪndʒ/
exhaust *v* /ɪɡˈzɔːst/
expectation *n* /ˌekspekˈteɪʃn/
expertise *n* /ˌekspɜːˈtiːz/
exploit *v* /ɪkˈsplɔɪt/
export *v* /ɪkˈspɔːt/
express *v* /ɪkˈspres/
fair *adj* /feə(r)/
fair *n* /feə(r)/
fair trade *n* /ˌfeə ˈtreɪd/
familiar *adj* /fəˈmɪliə(r)/
feelings *n pl* /ˈfiːlɪŋz/
figures *n pl* /ˈfɪɡəz/
finally *adv* /ˈfaɪnəli/
financial *adj* /faɪˈnænʃl/
fixed *adj* /fɪkst/
flaw *n* /flɔː/
focus on *v* /ˈfəʊkəs ɒn/
foodstuffs *n pl* /ˈfuːdstʌfs/
force *v* /fɔːs/
free trade *n* /ˌfriː ˈtreɪd/
gain *v* /ɡeɪn/
generalizations *n pl*
   /ˌdʒenrəlaɪzˈeɪʃnz/
globalization *n* /ˌɡləʊbəlaɪzˈeɪʃn/
gross domestic product (GDP) *n*
   /ˌɡrəʊs dəˌmestɪk ˈprɒdʌkt/
guaranteed *adj* /ˌɡærənˈtiːd/
illustrate *v* /ˈɪləstreɪt/
impact *n* /ˈɪmpækt/
import *v* /ɪmˈpɔːt/
improvement *n* /ɪmˈpruːvmənt/
in favour of *adj* /ɪn ˈfeɪvə(r) ɒv/
in order to /ɪn ˈɔːdə tu/
in particular /ˌɪn pəˈtɪkjələ(r)/
income *n* /ˈɪnkʌm/
inflated *adj* /ɪnˈfleɪtɪd/
insignificant *adj* /ˌɪnsɪɡˈnɪfɪkənt/
investment *n* /ɪnˈvestmənt/
judge *v* /dʒʌdʒ/
label *n* /ˈleɪbl/
labour force *n* /ˈleɪbə ˌfɔːs/
legal *adj* /ˈliːɡl/
local *adj* /ˈləʊkl/
maintain *v* /meɪnˈteɪn/
malaria *n* /məˈleəriə/
managerial *adj* /ˌmænəˈdʒɪəriəl/
minority *n* /maɪˈnɒrəti/
morally *adv* /ˈmɒrəli/
moreover *adv* /mɔːrˈəʊvə(r)/
movement (political) *n*
   /ˈmuːvmənt/
multiple *adj* /ˈmʌltɪpl/
naturally *adv* /ˈnætʃrəli/
neutral *adj* /ˈnjuːtrəl/
objective *n, adj* /əbˈdʒektɪv/
one-sided *adj* /ˌwʌn ˈsaɪdɪd/
opportunity *n* /ˌɒpəˈtʃuːnəti/
ordinary *adj* /ˈɔːdnri/
over-priced *adj* /ˌəʊvəˈpraɪsd/
packaging *n* /ˈpækɪdʒɪŋ/
particles *n pl* /ˈpɑːtɪklz/
past *n, adj* /pɑːst/
pay *n* /peɪ/
peak seasons *n pl* /ˈpiːk ˌsiːzənz/
per capita *adj* /ˌpɜː ˈkæpɪtə/

percentage *n* /pəˈsentɪdʒ/
point of view *n* /ˌpɔɪnt əv ˈvjuː/
policy *n* /ˈpɒləsi/
popular *adj* /ˈpɒpjulə(r)/
present *v* /prɪˈzent/
price *n* /praɪs/
pricing *n* /ˈpraɪsɪŋ/
probably *adv* /ˈprɒbəbli/
profit margin *n* /ˈprɒfɪt ˌmɑːdʒɪn/
proven *adj* /ˈpruːvn/
rapid *adj* /ˈræpɪd/
reduction *n* /rɪˈdʌkʃn/
relatively *adv* /ˈrelətɪvli/
remote *adj* /rɪˈməʊt/
responsible *adj* /rɪˈspɒnsəbl/
result in *v* /rɪˈzʌlt ɪn/
retail *n* /ˈriːteɪl/
retailer *n* /ˈriːteɪlə(r)/
rich *adj* /rɪtʃ/
sales *n* /seɪlz/
scientifically *adv* /ˌsaɪənˈtɪfɪkli/
seasons *n pl* /ˈsiːzənz/
seem *adv* /siːm/
serious *adj* /ˈsɪəriəs/
share *v* /ʃeə(r)/
similarly *adv* /ˈsɪmɪləli/
situation *n* /ˌsɪtʃuˈeɪʃn/
slight *adj* /slaɪt/
soil *n* /sɔɪl/
speculation *n* /ˌspekjuˈleɪʃn/
state *v* /steɪt/
stoppage *n* /ˈstɒpɪdʒ/
strict *adj* /strɪkt/
strike *v* /straɪk/
substantial *adj* /səbˈstænʃl/
substantially *adv* /səbˈstænʃəli/
successfully *adv* /səkˈsesfəli/
supporters *n pl* /səˈpɔːtəz/
supporting *adj* /səˈpɔːtɪŋ/
technical *adj* /ˈteknɪkl/
technological *adj* /ˌteknəˈlɒdʒɪkl/
tend to *adv* /ˈtend tə/
tendency *n* /ˈtendənsi/
term *n* /tɜːm/
thesis statement *n* /ˈθiːsɪs
   ˌsteɪtmənt/
tin *n* /tɪn/
total *n* /ˈtəʊtl/
tourism *n* /ˈtʊərɪzəm/
trades people *n pl* /ˈtreɪdz piːpl/
traditions *n pl* /trəˈdɪʃnz/
true *adj* /truː/
undoubtedly *adv* /ʌnˈdaʊtɪdli/
unfairly *adv* /ʌnˈfeəli/
unfortunately *adv* /ʌnˈfɔːtʃənətli/
varying *adj* /ˈveəriŋ/
village *n* /ˈvɪlɪdʒ/
wealthy *adj* /ˈwelθi/
widely *adv* /ˈwaɪdli/
win-win *adj* /ˌwɪnˈwɪn/
wish *v* /wɪʃ/
with reference to /wɪð ˈrefrəns tə/
world market *n* /ˌwɜːld ˈmɑːkɪt/

Unit 6

abandon *v* /ə'bændən/
accidentally *adv* /ˌæksɪ'dentəli/
achievements *n pl* /ə'tʃiːvmənts/
actively *adv* /'æktɪvli/
add *v* /æd/
admire *v* /əd'maɪə(r)/
adverbial *adj* /æd'vɜːbiəl/
afterlife *n* /'ɑːftəlaɪf/
ancient *adj* /'eɪnʃənt/
appropriately *adv* /ə'prəʊpriətli/
archaeological *adj* /ˌɑːkiə'lɒdʒɪkl/
archaeologists *n pl*
   /ˌɑːki'ɒlədʒɪsts/
archer *n* /'ɑːtʃə(r)/
armour *n* /'ɑːmə(r)/
army *n* /'ɑːmi/
arrange *v* /ə'reɪndʒ/
artwork *n* /'ɑːtwɜːk/
ash *n* /æʃ/
aside *adj* /ə'saɪd/
assemble *v* /ə'sembl/
attentively *adv* /ə'tentɪvli/
bake *v* /beɪk/
become *v* /bɪ'kʌm/
brief *adj* /'briːf/
burial place *n* /'beriəl ˌpleɪs/
bury *v* /'beri/
cautiously *adv* /'kɔːʃəsli/
clause *n* /klɔːz/
clay *n* /kleɪ/
clearly *adv* /'klɪəli/
collapse *v* /kə'læps/
completely *adv* /kəm'pliːtli/
complicated *adj* /'kɒmplɪkeɪtɪd/
conquer *v* /'kɒŋkə(r)/
conserve *v* /kən'sɜːv/
construct *v* /kən'strʌkt/
correctly *adv* /kə'rektli/
covered by *v* /'kʌvəd ˌbaɪ/
craftsmen *n* /'krɑːftsmən/
death *n* /deθ/
deserve *v* /dɪ'zɜːv/
display *n, v* /dɪs'pleɪ/
drawings *n pl* /'drɔːɪŋz/
educate *v* /'edʒukeɪt/
emperor *n* /'empərə(r)/
endeavour *n* /ɪn'devə(r)/
enemies *n* /'enəmiz/
entrance fee *n* /'entrəns ˌfiː/
equipped *adj* /ɪ'kwɪpt/
eventually *adv* /ɪ'ventʃuəli/
excavations *n pl* /ˌekskə'veɪʃnz/
exhibit *v* /ɪg'zɪbɪt/
exhibition *n* /ˌeksɪ'bɪʃn/
expand *v* /ɪk'spænd/
explanations *n pl* /ˌeksplə'neɪʃnz/
expose to *v* /ɪk'spəʊz tə/
extensive *adj* /ɪk'stensɪv/
extensively *adv* /ɪk'stensɪvli/
facial *adj* /'feɪʃl/
fairly *adv* /'feəli/
figures *n pl* /'fɪgəz/
fire *n* /faɪə(r)/
formation *n* /fɔː'meɪʃn/
fragment *n* /'frægmənt/
funding *n* /'fʌndɪŋ/

helicopter *n* /'helɪkɒptə(r)/
heritage *n* /'herɪtɪdʒ/
high up *prep* /ˌhaɪ 'ʌp/
highlighted *adj* /'haɪlaɪtɪd/
highpoint *n* /'haɪpɔɪnt/
historian *n* /hɪ'stɔːriən/
honour *n* /'ɒnə(r)/
illustrated *adj* /'ɪləstreɪtɪd/
imperial *adj* /ɪm'pɪəriəl/
impressive *adj* /ɪm'presɪv/
in addition /ˌɪn ə'dɪʃn/
inaccessible *adj* /ˌɪnæk'sesəbl/
inappropriate *adj* /ˌɪnə'prəʊpriət/
Inca *n* /'ɪŋkə/
indicate *v* /'ɪndɪkeɪt/
infinitive (grammar) *n* /ɪn'fɪnətɪv/
inscription *n* /ɪn'skrɪpʃn/
invade *v* /ɪn'veɪd/
irrelevant *adj* /ɪ'reləvənt/
ivory *n* /'aɪvəri/
knowledge *n* /'nɒlɪdʒ/
laboratories *n pl* /lə'bɒrətriz/
last *v* /lɑːst/
life-like *adj* /'laɪflaɪk/
life-sized *adj* /'laɪfsaɪzd/
linked *adj* /'lɪŋkt/
logical *adj* /'lɒdʒɪkl/
lucky *adj* /'lʌki/
magnificent *adj* /mæg'nɪfɪsənt/
major *adj* /'meɪdʒə(r)/
manuscript *n* /'mænjuskrɪpt/
methodically *adv* /mə'θɒdɪkli/
military *n* /'mɪlətri/
monument *n* /'mɒnjumənt/
mosaic *n* /məʊ'zeɪɪk/
museum *n* /mju:'ziːəm/
nearby *prep* /ˌnɪə'baɪ/
north *n* /nɔːθ/
objects *n pl* /'ɒbdʒekts/
occupy *v* /'ɒkjupaɪ/
optimistic *adj* /ˌɒptɪ'mɪstɪk/
order *n* /'ɔːdə(r)/
outstanding *adj* /aʊt'stændɪŋ/
palace *n* /'pæləs/
peel off *v* /ˌpiːl 'ɒf/
period (of time) *n* /'pɪəriəd/
pilot *n* /'paɪlət/
position *n* /pə'zɪʃn/
precision *n* /prɪ'sɪʒn/
preserved *adj* /prɪ'zɜːvd/
president *n* /'prezɪdənt/
primary *adj* /'praɪməri/
production line *n* /prə'dʌkʃn
   ˌlaɪn/
protect *v* /prə'tekt/
province *n* /'prɒvɪns/
rank *n* /ræŋk/
rebuilt *v* /ˌriː'bɪlt/
recall *v* /rɪ'kɔːl/
reconstruct *v* /ˌriːkən'strʌkt/
rediscover *v* /ˌriːdɪs'kʌvə(r)/
regional *adj* /'riːdʒənl/
relate to *v* /rɪ'leɪt tə/
remarkably *adj* /rɪ'mɑːkəbli/
repair *v* /rɪ'peə(r)/
resignation *n* /ˌrezɪg'neɪʃn/
revenue *n* /'revənjuː/
ruin *n* /'ruːɪn/

rulers *n pl* /'ruːləz/
scan *v* /skæn/
scientific *adj* /ˌsaɪən'tɪfɪk/
settlement *n* /'setlmənt/
several *adv* /'sevrəl/
sharply *adv* /'ʃɑːpli/
sink *v* /sɪŋk/
soldiers *n pl* /'səʊldʒəz/
solution *n* /sə'luːʃn/
south *n* /saʊθ/
speculate *v* /'spekjuleɪt/
statues *n pl* /'stætʃuːz/
steadily *adv* /'stedɪli/
storage *n* /'stɔːrɪdʒ/
surround *v* /sə'raʊnd/
temples *n pl* /'templz/
terracotta *n, adj* /ˌterə'kɒtə/
thriving *adj* /'θraɪvɪŋ/
tomb *n* /tuːm/
undamaged *adj* /ˌʌn'dæmɪdʒd/
uniforms *n pl* /'juːnɪfɔːmz/
united *adj* /ju'naɪtɪd/
various *adj* /'veəriəs/
violent *adj* /'vaɪələnt/
volcanic *adj* /vɒl'kænɪk/
wealthy *adj* /'welθi/
website *n* /'websaɪt/
workers *n pl* /'wɜːkəz/

Unit 7

a series of *n* /ə 'sɪəriːz əv/
accommodation *n* /əˌkɒmə'deɪʃn/
acknowledge *v* /ək'nɒlɪʤ/
addition *n* /ə'dɪʃn/
amazing *adj* /ə'meɪzɪŋ/
amount *n* /ə'maʊnt/
appear *v* /ə'pɪə(r)/
architect *n* /'ɑːkɪtekt/
architectural *adj* /ˌɑːkɪ'tektʃərəl/
area *n* /'eərɪə/
artificial *adj* /ˌɑːtɪ'fɪʃl/
astonishing *adj* /ə'stɒnɪʃɪŋ/
author *n* /'ɔːθə(r)/
base *n* /beɪs/
bibliography *n* /ˌbɪbli'ɒgrəfi/
blood *n* /blʌd/
break (a record) *v* /breɪk/
breakwater *n* /'breɪkwɔːtə(r)/
bridge *n* /brɪʤ/
ceremony *n* /'serəməni/
challenging *adj* /'tʃælɪnʤɪŋ/
classical *adj* /'klæsɪkl/
coastline *n* /'kəʊstlaɪn/
combine with *v* /'kəmbaɪn ˌwɪð/
common *n* /'kɒmən/
congestion *n* /kən'ʤestʃn/
consideration *n* /kənˌsɪdə'reɪʃn/
consist of *v* /kən'sɪst əv/
construct *v* /kən'strʌkt/
constructions *n pl* /kən'strʌkʃnz/
continents *n pl* /'kɒntɪnənts/
continuing *adj* /kən'tɪnjuɪŋ/
controversial *adj* /ˌkɒntrə'vɜːʃl/
conventions *n pl* /kən'venʃnz/
crash-land *v* /'kræʃ lænd/
credit *v* /'kredɪt/
crew *n* /kruː/
cubic *adj* /'kjuːbɪk/
culture *n* /'kʌltʃə(r)/
dam *n* /dæm/
debris *n* /'debriː/
decade *n* /'dekeɪd/
desert *n* /'dezət/
design *n* /dɪ'zaɪn/
dominate *v* /'dɒmɪneɪt/
during *adv* /'ʤʊərɪŋ/
efficient *adj* /ɪ'fɪʃnt/
employ *v* /ɪm'plɔɪ/
energy *n* /'enəʤi/
engineering *n* /ˌenʤɪ'nɪərɪŋ/
engineers *n pl* /ˌenʤɪ'nɪəz/
entertainment *n* /ˌentə'teɪnmənt/
environmental *adj*
    /ɪnˌvaɪrən'mentl/
equivalent *n* /ɪ'kwɪvələnt/
estates *n pl* /ɪ'steɪts/
estimate *v* /'estɪmeɪt/
existing *adj* /ɪg'zɪstɪŋ/
expansion *n* /ɪk'spænʃn/
extend *v* /ɪk'stend/
extreme *adj* /ɪk'striːm/
facilities *n pl* /fə'sɪlətiz/
fireworks *n pl* /'faɪəwɜːks/
flow *v* /fləʊ/
forecasters *n pl* /'fɔːkɑːstəz/
function *v* /'fʌŋkʃn/

giant *adj* /'ʤaɪənt/
gravitational *adj* /ˌgrævɪ'teɪʃənl/
ground control *n* /'graʊnd
    kən,trəʊl/
height *n* /haɪt/
high-rise *n* /'haɪraɪz/
high-speed *adj* /ˌhaɪ 'spiːd/
horizontally *adv* /ˌhɒrɪ'zɒntəli/
hydroelectric *adj*
    /ˌhaɪdrəʊɪ'lektrɪk/
impressive *adj* /ɪm'presɪv/
inaugurate *v* /ɪn'ɔːgjəreɪt/
incorporate *v* /ɪn'kɔːpəreɪt/
increase *n* /'ɪnkriːs/
influence *n* /'ɪnfluəns/
initially *adv* /ɪ'nɪʃəli/
initials *n pl* /ɪ'nɪʃlz/
innovative *adj* /'ɪnəvətɪv/
instantly *adv* /'ɪnstəntli/
Islamic *adj* /ɪz'læmɪk/
islands *n pl* /'aɪləndz/
issues *n pl* /'ɪʃuːz/
joint *adj* /ʤɔɪnt/
land *n* /lænd/
launch *v* /lɔːntʃ/
leisure *n* /'leʒə(r)/
length *n* /leŋθ/
lifts *n pl* /lɪfts/
limitless *adj* /'lɪmɪtləs/
line (train) *n* /laɪn/
linked by *adj* /'lɪŋkt baɪ/
luxury *n* /'lʌkʃəri/
make sense *v* /ˌmeɪk 'sens/
make up *v* /ˌmeɪk 'ʌp/
man-made *adj* /ˌmæn'meɪd/
marinas *n pl* /mə'riːnəz/
meteorlogical *adj*
    /ˌmiːtɪərə'lɒʤɪkl/
mission *n* /'mɪʃn/
necessary *v* /'nesəsəri/
noticeable *adj* /'nəʊtɪsəbl/
observations *n pl* /ˌɒbzə'veɪʃnz/
obtain *v* /əb'teɪn/
on sale *adj* /ˌɒn 'seɪl/
orbit *v* /'ɔːbɪt/
overcrowding *n* /ˌəʊvə'kraʊdɪŋ/
pass *v* /pɑːs/
performance *n* /pə'fɔːməns/
phenomena *n* /fə'nɒmɪnə/
predict *v* /prɪ'dɪkt/
privately-owned *adj* /'praɪvətli
    ˌəʊnd/
project *n* /'prɒʤekt/
pronouns *n pl* /'prəʊnaʊnz/
publisher *n* /'pʌblɪʃə(r)/
pull back *v* /ˌpʊl 'bæk/
rail *n* /reɪl/
railway *n* /'reɪlweɪ/
reach *v* /'riːtʃ/
reclaim *v* /rɪ'kleɪm/
recognizable *adj* /'rekəgnaɪzɪəbl/
referencing *n* /'refrənsɪŋ/
reflect *v* /rɪ'flekt/
rehearsal *n* /rɪ'hɜːsl/
remarkable *adj* /rɪ'mɑːkəbl/
repetition *n* /ˌrepəɪ'tɪʃn/
residential *adj* /ˌrezɪ'denʃl/
resorts *n pl* /rɪ'zɔːts/

retrieval *n* /rɪ'triːvl/
retrieve *v* /rɪ'triːv/
roof *n* /ruːf/
safety *n* /'seɪfti/
safety measures *n* /'seɪfti ˌmeʒəz/
sample *n* /'sɑːmpl/
sand *n* /sænd/
seismic *adj* /'saɪzmɪk/
severe *adj* /sɪ'vɪə(r)/
shape *n* /ʃeɪp/
size *n* /saɪz/
skyline *n* /'skaɪlaɪn/
skyscrapers *n pl* /'skaɪskreɪpəz/
sleepiness *n* /'sliːpɪnəs/
slender *adj* /'slendə(r)/
solar *adj* /'səʊlə(r)/
solar system *n* /'səʊlə(r) ˌsɪstəm/
sophisticated *adj* /sə'fɪstɪkeɪtɪd/
space *n* /speɪs/
spectacular *adj* /spek'tækjələ(r)/
stilts *n pl* /stɪltz/
structural *adj* /'strʌktʃərəl/
structures *n pl* /'strʌktʃəz/
studios *n pl* /'stjuːdiəʊz/
successfully *adv* /sʌk'sesfəli/
suffixes *n pl* /'sʌfɪksɪz/
sustain *v* /sə'steɪn/
symbolize *v* /'sɪmbəlaɪz/
televise *v* /'teləvaɪz/
theorize *v* /'θɪəraɪz/
ton *n* /tʌn/
tourist attraction *n* /'tʊərɪst
    ə,trækʃn/
tunnel *n* /'tʌnl/
undoubtedly *adv* /ʌn'daʊtɪdli/
unnecessarily *adv* /ˌʌn'nesəsərəli/
unquestionably *adv*
    /ˌʌn'kwestʃənəbli/
vehicles *n pl* /'viːəklz/
vertically *adv* /'vɜːtɪkli/
volume (book) *n* /'vɒljuːm/
wheel *n* /wiːl/
withstand *v* /wɪð'stænd/
wonders *n pl* /'wʌndəz/

Unit 8

act of n /ˈækt əv/
address v /əˈdres/
adequate adj /ˈædɪkwət/
adopt v /əˈdɒpt/
advertise v /ˈædvətaɪz/
advertising n /ˈædvətaɪzɪŋ/
afterwards prep /ˈɑːftəwədz/
allow v /əˈlaʊ/
already adv /ɔːlˈredi/
although adv /ɔːlˈðəʊ/
announce v /əˈnaʊns/
antonym n /ˈæntənɪm/
arrangements n pl
    /əˈreɪndʒmənts/
athletes n pl /ˈæθliːts/
attract v /əˈtrækt/
audiences n pl /ˈɔːdiənsɪz/
avoid v /əˈvɔɪd/
award v /əˈwɔːd/
aware of /əˈweə(r) əv/
bid n /bɪd/
blunt adj /blʌnt/
brackets n pl /ˈbrækɪts/
broadcast v /ˈbrɔːdkɑːst/
broadcasting rights n pl
    /ˈbrɔːdkɑːstɪŋ ˌraɪts/
budget n /ˈbʌdʒɪt/
burden n /ˈbɜːdən/
busy adj /ˈbɪzi/
cafeteria n /ˌkæfəˈtɪəriə/
camp v /kæmp/
capital adj /ˈkæpɪtl/
catering n /ˈkeɪtərɪŋ/
charity n /ˈtʃærəti/
citizen n /ˈsɪtɪzn/
claim v /kleɪm/
clearly adv /ˈklɪəli/
committee n /kəˈmɪti/
compete v /kəmˈpiːt/
competition n /ˌkɒmpəˈtɪʃn/
considerable adj /kənˈsɪdrəbl/
context n /ˈkɒntekst/
conversation n /ˌkɒnvəˈseɪʃn/
cover v /ˈkʌvə(r)/
create v /kriˈeɪt/
danger n /ˈdeɪndʒə(r)/
decision n /dɪˈsɪʒn/
department n /dɪˈpɑːtmənt/
despite adv /dɪˈspaɪt/
destinations n pl /ˌdestɪˈneɪʃnz/
diagram n /ˈdaɪəgræm/
disagreement n /ˌdɪsəˈgriːmənt/
disruption n /dɪsˈrʌpʃn/
distribution n /ˌdɪstrɪˈbjuːʃn/
draw n /drɔː/
earn v /ɜːn/
employment n /ɪmˈplɔɪmənt/
enable v /ɪˈneɪbl/
enormous adj /ɪˈnɔːməs/
enter v /ˈentə(r)/
even adj /ˈiːvn/
event n /ɪˈvent/
everyday adj /ˈevrideɪ/
exact adj /ɪgˈzækt/
exist v /ɪgˈzɪst/
fall on v /ˈfɔːl ɒn/

fiercely adv /ˈfɪəsli/
finance n /ˈfaɪnæns/
financial adj /faɪˈnænʃl/
fundamental adj /ˌfʌndəˈmentl/
funding n /ˈfʌndɪŋ/
funds n pl /fʌndz/
gain v /geɪn/
give rise to v /ˌgɪv ˈraɪz tə/
global adj /ˈgləʊbl/
governing body n /ˌgʌvənɪŋ
    ˈbɒdi/
ground n /graʊnd/
historical adj /hɪˈstɒrɪkl/
hospitality n /ˌhɒspɪˈtæləti/
host v /həʊst/
huge adj /hjuːdʒ/
improvements n pl
    /ɪmˈpruːvmənts/
in spite of /ɪn ˈspaɪt əv/
in terms of /ɪn ˈtɜːmz əv/
increase v /ɪnˈkriːs/
inevitable adj /ɪnˈevɪtəbl/
inferior adj /ɪnˈfɪəriə(r)/
inflation n /ɪnˈfleɪʃn/
infrastructure n /ˈɪnfrəstrʌktʃə(r)/
invest v /ɪnˈvest/
invite v /ɪnˈvaɪt/
involved adj /ɪnˈvɒlvd/
knife n /naɪf/
large adj /lɑːdʒ/
last v /lɑːst/
later adv /ˈleɪtə(r)/
long lasting adj /ˌlɒŋ ˈlɑːstɪŋ/
look out for v /lʊk ˈaʊt fə/
lucrative adj /ˈluːkrətɪv/
manpower n /ˈmænpaʊə(r)/
map n /mæp/
marketing n /ˈmɑːkɪtɪŋ/
match n /mætʃ/
mention v /ˈmenʃn/
middle adj /ˈmɪdl/
multinational adj /ˌmʌltiˈnæʃnəl/
needs n pl /niːdz/
networks n pl /ˈnetwɜːks/
nevertheless adv /ˌnevəðəˈles/
normal adj /ˈnɔːml/
note-taking n /ˈnəʊt ˌteɪkɪŋ/
occasion n /əˈkeɪʒn/
odd adj /ɒd/
operate v /ˈɒpəreɪt/
origins n pl /ˈɒrɪdʒɪnz/
outweigh v /aʊtˈweɪ/
overheads n pl /ˈəʊvəhedz/
patient n /ˈpeɪʃnt/
per cent n /pəˈsent/
permanent adj /ˈpɜːmənənt/
permission n /pəˈmɪʃn/
personalities n pl /ˌpɜːsəˈnælətiz/
pitch n /pɪtʃ/
possibility n /ˌpɒsəˈbɪləti/
promotion n /prəˈməʊʃn/
proportion n /prəˈpɔːʃn/
publication n /ˌpʌblɪˈkeɪʃn/
quote v /kwəʊt/
raise v /reɪz/
real adj /rɪəl/
redundancy n /rɪˈdʌndənsi/
rent v /rent/

requirements n pl
    /rɪˈkwaɪəmənts/
resign v /rɪˈzaɪn/
respect n /rɪˈspekt/
reuse v /ˌriːˈjuːz/
revenues n pl /ˈrevənjuːz/
rights n pl /raɪts/
rings n pl /rɪŋz/
security n /sɪˈkjʊərəti/
slot n /slɒt/
sociology n /ˌsəʊsiˈɒlədʒi/
sponsor v /ˈspɒnsə(r)/
sponsors n pl /ˈspɒnsəz/
sponsorship n /ˈspɒnsəʃɪp/
stadium n /ˈsteɪdiəm/
state v /steɪt/
statement n /ˈsteɪtmənt/
sufficient adj /səˈfɪʃnt/
sum (of money) n /sʌm/
support v /səˈpɔːt/
symbol n /ˈsɪmbl/
take into consideration /ˌteɪk ɪntə
    kənsɪdəˈreɪʃn/
take place v /ˌteɪk ˈpleɪs/
taxes n pl /ˈtæksɪz/
televise v /ˈtelɪvaɪz/
ticket n /ˈtɪkɪt/
transmit v /trænsˈmɪt/
underpaid adj /ˌʌndəˈpeɪd/
unexpected adj /ˌʌnɪkˈspektɪd/
unskilled adj /ˌʌnˈskɪld/
upgrade v /ˌʌpˈgreɪd/
upgrade n /ˈʌpgreɪd/
vaccination n /ˌvæksɪˈneɪʃn/
valuable adj /ˈvæljuəbl/
view v /vjuː/
vigilance n /ˈvɪdʒɪləns/
visitors n pl /ˈvɪzɪtəz/
voluntary adj /ˈvɒləntri/
walk off v /ˌwɔːk ˈɒf/
weak adj /wiːk/
welcome v, n /ˈwelkəm/
wide-reaching adj /ˌwaɪd ˈriːtʃɪŋ/
win v /wɪn/
world-class adj /ˌwɜːldˈklɑːs/

Unit 9

a tenth *n* /ə 'tenθ/
academic year *n* /ˌækədemɪk 'jɪə(r)/
actually *adv* /'æktʃuəli/
age *n* /eɪʤ/
agriculture *n* /'ægrɪkʌltʃə(r)/
approximately *adv* /ə'prɒksɪmətli/
around *prep* /ə'raʊnd/
automation *n* /ˌɔ:tə'meɪʃn/
bacteria *n* /bæk'tɪərɪə/
bar chart *n* /'bɑ: tʃɑ:t/
between *prep* /bɪ'twi:n/
bilateral *adj* /ˌbaɪ'lætərəl/
biochemistry *n* /ˌbaɪəʊ'kemɪstri/
candidate *n* /'kændɪdət/
clarify *v* /'klærɪfaɪ/
comparisons *n pl* /kəm'pærɪsnz/
composite *n* /'kɒmpəzɪt/
considerably *adv* /kən'sɪdrəbli/
constantly *adv* /'kɒnstəntli/
consultancy *n* /kən'sʌltənsi/
contain *v* /kən'teɪn/
critics *n* /'krɪtɪks/
data *n* /'deɪtə/
decline *v* /dɪ'klaɪn/
decrease *v* /dɪ'kri:s/
decrease *n* /'di:kri:s/
dentistry *n* /'dentɪstri/
describe *v* /dɪ'skraɪb/
description *n* /dɪ'skrɪpʃn/
disorganized *adj* /dɪs'ɔ:gənaɪzd/
distribution *n* /ˌdɪstrɪ'bju:ʃn/
dramatic *adj* /drə'mætɪk/
dramatically *adv* /drə'mætɪkli/
drop by *v* /ˌdrɒp 'baɪ/
economists *n pl* /ɪ'kɒnəmɪsts/
employees *n pl* /ɪm'plɔii:z/
enable *v* /ɪ'neɪbl/
enrol *v* /ɪn'rəʊl/
enrolments *n pl* /ɪn'rəʊlmənts/
equivalent *n* /ɪ'kwɪvələnt/
estimate *v* /'estɪmeɪt/
explore *v* /ɪk'splɔ:(r)/
faculties *n pl* /'fækəltiz/
fall *v* /fɔ:l/
female *n* /'fi:meɪl/
figures *n pl* /'fɪgəz/
fluctuate *v* /'flʌktjueɪt/
fungi *n* /'fʌngi:/
future *n* /'fju:tʃə(r)/
globally *adv* /'gləʊbəli/
go down *v* /ˌgəʊ 'daʊn/
go up *v* /ˌgəʊ 'ʌp/
graduate *n* /'græʤuət/
gram *n* /græm/
graphics *n pl* /'græfɪks/
grow *v* /grəʊ/
hand in *v* /ˌhænd 'ɪn/
happen *v* /'hæpn/
higher education *n* /ˌhaɪə(r) edju'keɪʃn/
illegible *adj* /ɪ'leʤəbl/
illustrate *v* /'ɪləstreɪt/
impact *n* /'ɪmpækt/
imperfect *adj* /ɪm'pɜ:fɪkt/
in fact /ɪn 'fækt/

increase *v* /ɪn'kri:s/
increase *n* /'ɪnkri:s/
industrialization *n* /ɪnˌdʌstrɪəlaɪ'zeɪʃn/
industry *n* /'ɪndəstri/
instrument *n* /'ɪnstrəmənt/
insurance *n* /ɪn'ʃʊərəns/
interpret *v* /ɪn'tɜ:prɪt/
intranet *n* /'ɪntrənet/
IT (information technology) *n* /ˌaɪ ti ˌɪnfəˌmeɪʃn tek'nɒləʤi/
just over /ˌʤʌst 'əʊvə(r)/
kilometres *n pl* /kɪ'lɒmɪtəz/
lead up to *v* /ˌli:d 'ʌp tə/
legal *adj* /'li:gl/
level out *v* /ˌlevl 'aʊt/
line graph *n* /'laɪn ˌgrɑ:f/
living *adj* /'lɪvɪŋ/
main *adj* /meɪn/
male *n* /meɪl/
marginal *adj* /'mɑ:ʤɪnl/
marginally *adv* /'mɑ:ʤɪnəli/
means of *n* /'mi:nz əv/
media *n* /'mi:dɪə/
million *n* /'mɪljən/
modify *v* /'mɒdɪfaɪ/
monorail *n* /'mɒnəʊreɪl/
multilingual *adj* /ˌmʌlti'lɪŋgwəl/
nanosecond *n* /'nænəʊsekənd/
nearly *adv* /'nɪəli/
notice *v* /'nəʊtɪs/
noticeable *adj* /'nəʊtɪsəbl/
noticeably *adv* /'nəʊtɪsəbli/
numerical *adj* /nju:'merɪkl/
office *n* /'ɒfɪs/
particularly *adv* /pə'tɪkjələli/
patterns *n pl* /'pætənz/
per cent *n* /pə 'sent/
percentage *n* /pə'sentɪʤ/
photosynthesis *n* /ˌfəʊtəʊ'sɪnθəsɪs/
pie chart *n* /'paɪ tʃɑ:t/
plants *n pl* /plɑ:nts/
plummet *v* /'plʌmɪt/
plunge *v* /plʌnʤ/
postgraduate *n* /ˌpəʊst'græʤuət/
predict *v* /prɪ'dɪkt/
prefixes *n pl* /'pri:fɪksɪz/
prepositions *n pl* /ˌprepə'zɪʃnz/
preview *v* /'pri:vju:/
process *n* /'prəʊses/
public services *n pl* /ˌpʌblɪk 'sɜ:vɪsɪz/
quarters *n pl* /'kwɔ:təz/
radically *adv* /'rædɪkli/
reach a peak *v* /ˌri:tʃ ə 'pi:k/
recession *n* /rɪ'seʃn/
reduce *v* /rɪ'dju:s/
reflect *v* /rɪ'flekt/
remember *v* /rɪ'membə(r)/
represent *v* /ˌreprɪ'zent/
reread *v* /ˌri:'ri:d/
rise *v* /raɪz/
rocket *v* /'rɒkɪt/
sectors *n pl* /'sektəz/
services *n pl* /'sɜ:vɪsɪz/
service-sector *n* /'sɜ:vɪs ˌsektə(r)/

show *v* /ʃəʊ/
similarly *adv* /'sɪmɪləli/
slight *adj* /slaɪt/
slightly *adv* /'slaɪtli/
soar *v* /sɔ:(r)/
social work *n* /ˌsəʊʃl 'wɜ:k/
stabilize *v* /'steɪbəlaɪz/
statistical *adj* /stə'tɪstɪkl/
statistics *n pl* /stə'tɪstɪks/
steadily *adv* /'stedɪli/
steady *adj* /'stedi/
subject *n* /'sʌbʤekt/
submarine *n* /ˌsʌbmə'ri:n/
sub-sector *n* /'sʌbˌsektə(r)/
substantial *adj* /səb'stænʃl/
subtitles *n* /'sʌbtaɪtlz/
such as /'sʌtʃ əz/
tendencies *n pl* /'tendənsiz/
textile *n* /'tekstaɪl/
the same *pron* /ðə 'seɪm/
trade *n, v* /treɪd/
transform *v* /træns'fɔ:m/
trends *n pl* /trendz/
twice as many /ˌtwaɪs əz 'meni/
undergraduates *n pl* /ˌʌndə'græʤuəts/
upward *prep* /'ʌpwəd/
values *n pl* /'vælju:z/
varied *adj* /'veərid/
wages *n pl* /'weɪʤɪz/
whole *n* /həʊl/
workforce *n* /'wɜ:kfɔ:s/

Unit 10

abbreviations *n pl* /ə,bri:vi'eɪʃnz/
accents *n pl* /'æksents/
access *n* /'ækses/
accommodate *v* /ə'kɒmədeɪt/
ad hoc *adj* /,æd 'hɒk/
adapter *n* /ə'dæptə(r)/
advisable *adj* /əd'vaɪzəbl/
amplifiers *n pl* /'æmplɪfaɪəz/
antenna *n* /æn'tenə/
attach *v* /ə'tætʃ/
battery *n* /'bætri/
bell *n* /bel/
birth *n* /bɜ:θ/
booth *n* /bu:ð/
bring back *v* /,brɪŋ 'bæk/
broad *adj* /brɔ:d/
card *n* /kɑ:d/
carrier pigeon *n* /'kæriə pɪdʒɪn/
centre *n* /'sentə(r)/
certain *adv* /'sɜ:tn/
certificate *n* /sə'tɪfɪkət/
circuit *n* /'sɜ:kɪt/
clarify *v* /'klærɪfaɪ/
code *n* /kəʊd/
collect *v* /kə'lekt/
communication *n*
   /kə,mju:nɪ'keɪʃn/
comparison *n* /kəm'pærɪsn/
complete *v* /kəm'pli:t/
conclude *v* /kən'klu:d/
connect *v* /kə'nekt/
consecutive *adj* /kən'sekjətɪv/
consider *v* /kən'sɪdə(r)/
continents *n pl* /'kɒntɪnənts/
deal with *v* /'di:l wɪð/
decode *v* /,di:'kəʊd/
decrease *v* /dɪ'kri:s/
degree *n* /dɪ'gri:/
devices *n pl* /dɪ'vaɪsɪz/
dialects *n pl* /'daɪəlekts/
digital *adj* /'dɪdʒɪtl/
digitalized *adj* /'dɪdʒɪtəlaɪzd/
director *n* /daɪ'rektə(r)/
doubt *n* /daʊt/
ease *n* /i:z/
entertainment *n* /,entə'taɪnmənt/
equally *adv* /'i:kwəli/
era *n* /'ɪərə/
eruption *n* /ɪ'rʌpʃn/
estimates *n pl* /'estɪməts/
everywhere *adv* /'evriweə(r)/
express *v* /ɪk'spres/
fit *v* /fɪt/
flag *n* /flæg/
fluent *adj* /'flu:ənt/
force *v* /fɔ:s/
foreign *adj* /'fɒrən/
formal *adj* /'fɔ:ml/
gather *v* /'gæðə(r)/
generation *n* /,dʒenə'reɪʃn/
get in touch with /,get ɪn 'tʌtʃ
   wɪð/
go down *v* /,gəʊ 'daʊn/
guesses *n pl* /'gesɪz/
hall *n* /hɔ:l/
homes *n pl* /həʊmz/

hotspots *n pl* /'hɒtspɒts/
idea *n* /aɪ'dɪə/
illness *n* /'ɪl'nəs/
images *n pl* /'ɪmɪdʒɪz/
in addition to /ɪn ə'dɪʃn tə/
informal *adj* /ɪn'fɔ:ml/
institutions *n pl* /,ɪnstɪ'tju:ʃnz/
interpret *v* /ɪn'tɜ:prɪt/
interpreter *n* /ɪn'tɜ:prɪtə(r)/
invention *n* /ɪn'venʃn/
inventors *n pl* /ɪn'ventəz/
keep up to date with /,ki:p ʌp tə
   'deɪt wɪð/
launch *v* /lɔ:ntʃ/
legal *adj* /'li:gl/
library *n* /'laɪbrəri/
literally *adv* /'lɪtərəli/
local *adj* /'ləʊkl/
long-distance *adj* /,lɒŋ'dɪstəns/
look like *v* /'lʊk ,laɪk/
mastery *n* /'mɑ:stəri/
meeting *n* /'mi:tɪŋ/
membership *n* /'membəʃɪp/
microphone *n* /'maɪkrəfəʊn/
minimum *adj* /'mɪnɪməm/
mirrors *n pl* /'mɪrəz/
miss *v* /mɪs/
mother tongue *n* /'mʌðə ,tʌŋ/
move *v* /mu:v/
multi-functions *n pl*
   /,mʌlti'fʌŋkʃnz/
multiple *adj* /'mʌltɪpl/
oral *adj* /'ɔ:rəl/
payment *n* /'peɪmənt/
pocket-sized *adj* /'pɒkɪtsaɪzd/
portable *adj* /'pɔ:təbl/
positioning *n* /pə'zɪʃənɪŋ/
postpone *v* /pəʊst'pəʊn/
practices *n pl* /'præktɪsɪz/
preferable *adj* /'prefrəbl/
presentations *n pl* /,prezn'teɪʃnz/
presenter *n* /prɪ'zentə(r)/
press *v* /pres/
probable *adj* /'prɒbəbl/
project *v* /prə'dʒekt/
protocols *n pl* /'prəʊtəkɒlz/
provider *n* /prə'vaɪdə(r)/
put (sth) off *v* /,pʊt 'ɒf/
radio *n* /'reɪdiəʊ/
radio waves *n pl* /'reɪdiəʊ weɪvz/
rapid *adj* /'ræpɪd/
recap *v* /'ri:kæp/
recover *v* /rɪ'kʌvə(r)/
region *n* /'ri:dʒən/
represent *v* /,reprɪ'zent/
requirements *n pl*
   /rɪ'kwaɪəmənts/
resemble *v* /rɪ'zembl/
residents *n pl* /'rezɪdənts/
revolution *n* /,revə'lu:ʃn/
role *n* /rəʊl/
schedule *n* /'ʃedju:l/
screens *n pl* /skri:nz/
seconds *n pl* /'sekəndz/
semaphore *n* /'seməfɔ:(r)/
send *v* /send/
sign languages *n pl* /'saɪn
   ,læŋgwɪdʒɪz/

signal *n* /'sɪgnəl/
signalling *n* /'sɪgnəlɪŋ/
signed *adj* /saɪnd/
simultaneous *adj* /,sɪml'teɪniəs/
sink *v* /sɪŋk/
situation *n* /,sɪtʃu:'eɪʃn/
smart *adj* /smɑ:t/
speaker *n* /'spi:kə(r)/
speech *n* /'spi:tʃ/
stand for *v* /'stænd fə/
stocks and shares *n* /,stɒks n
   'ʃeəz/
take ages /,teɪk 'eɪdʒɪz/
talk *n* /tɔ:k/
telecommunication *n*
   /,telɪkə,mju:nɪ'keɪʃn/
telegraph *n* /'telɪgrɑ:f/
text *v* /tekst/
theory *n* /'θɪəri/
three-dimensional *adj*
   /,θri:daɪ'menʃənl/
time-consuming *adj*
   /'taɪmkənsju:mɪŋ/
tiny *adj* /'taɪni/
tongue *n* /tʌŋ/
training *n* /'treɪnɪŋ/
transactions *n pl* /trænz'ækʃnz/
transatlantic *adj* /,trænzət'læntɪk/
translate *v* /træn'sleɪt/
translation *n* /træns'leɪʃn/
transmit *v* /træns'mɪt/
truly *adv* /'tru:li/
tuners *n pl* /'tju:nəz/
type *n* /taɪp/
typewriters *n pl* /'taɪpraɪtəz/
undergo *v* /ʌndə'gəʊ/
via *prep* /'vaɪə/
videoconferencing *n*
   /'vɪdiəʊkɒnfərənsɪŋ/
whisper *v* /'wɪspə(r)/
widespread *adj* /'waɪdspred/
wireless *adj* /'waɪələs/
with *prep* /wɪð/

PHONETIC SYMBOLS

Consonants				
1	/p/	as in	**pen**	/pen/
2	/b/	as in	**big**	/bɪg/
3	/t/	as in	**tea**	/ti:/
4	/d/	as in	**do**	/du:/
5	/k/	as in	**cat**	/kæt/
6	/g/	as in	**go**	/gəʊ/
7	/f/	as in	**four**	/fɔ:/
8	/v/	as in	**very**	/'veri/
9	/s/	as in	**son**	/sʌn/
10	/z/	as in	**zoo**	/zu:/
11	/l/	as in	**live**	/lɪv/
12	/m/	as in	**my**	/maɪ/
13	/n/	as in	**near**	/nɪə/
14	/h/	as in	**happy**	/'hæpi/
15	/r/	as in	**red**	/red/
16	/j/	as in	**yes**	/jes/
17	/w/	as in	**want**	/wɒnt/
18	/θ/	as in	**thanks**	/θæŋks/
19	/ð/	as in	**the**	/ðə/
20	/ʃ/	as in	**she**	/ʃi:/
21	/ʒ/	as in	**television**	/'telɪvɪʒn/
22	/tʃ/	as in	**child**	/tʃaɪld/
23	/dʒ/	as in	**German**	/'dʒɜ:mən/
24	/ŋ/	as in	**English**	/'ɪŋglɪʃ/

Vowels				
25	/i:/	as in	**see**	/si:/
26	/ɪ/	as in	**his**	/hɪz/
27	/i/	as in	**twenty**	/'twenti/
28	/e/	as in	**ten**	/ten/
29	/æ/	as in	**stamp**	/stæmp/
30	/ɑ:/	as in	**father**	/'fɑ:ðə/
31	/ɒ/	as in	**hot**	/hɒt/
32	/ɔ:/	as in	**morning**	/'mɔ:nɪŋ/
33	/ʊ/	as in	**football**	/'fʊtbɔ:l/
34	/u:/	as in	**you**	/ju:/
35	/ʌ/	as in	**sun**	/sʌn/
36	/ɜ:/	as in	**learn**	/lɜ:n/
37	/ə/	as in	**letter**	/'letə/

Diphthongs (two vowels together)				
38	/eɪ/	as in	**name**	/neɪm/
39	/əʊ/	as in	**no**	/nəʊ/
40	/aɪ/	as in	**my**	/maɪ/
41	/aʊ/	as in	**how**	/haʊ/
42	/ɔɪ/	as in	**boy**	/bɔɪ/
43	/ɪə/	as in	**hear**	/hɪə/
44	/eə/	as in	**where**	/weə/
45	/ʊə/	as in	**tour**	/tʊə/

OXFORD
UNIVERSITY PRESS

Great Clarendon Street, Oxford OX2 6DP

Oxford University Press is a department of the University of Oxford.
It furthers the University's objective of excellence in research, scholarship,
and education by publishing worldwide in

Oxford New York

Auckland Cape Town Dar es Salaam Hong Kong Karachi
Kuala Lumpur Madrid Melbourne Mexico City Nairobi
New Delhi Shanghai Taipei Toronto

With offices in

Argentina Austria Brazil Chile Czech Republic France Greece
Guatemala Hungary Italy Japan Poland Portugal Singapore
South Korea Switzerland Thailand Turkey Ukraine Vietnam

OXFORD and OXFORD ENGLISH are registered trade marks of
Oxford University Press in the UK and in certain other countries

ISBN: 978 0 19 471576 8

Printed in China

ACKNOWLEDGEMENTS

*We would like to thank the following for permission to reproduce the following
photographs*: Action Plus p66 (Haile Gebrselassie/Glyn Kirk); Alamy Images
pp6 (school children/John Sturrock), 7 (Venezuelan classroom/Chad Ehlers),
11 (books/Chris Stock (photography)), 15 (pills/WoodyStock), 19 (broccoli/
foodfolio), 20 (Curitiba, Brazil/Marcelo Rudini), 28 (dripping tap/Arcaid), 35
(wind turbines/Cliff LeSergent), 38 (fairtrade peeled banana/Darren Matthews),
38 (fairtrade coffee/Helene Rogers), 40 (Peru coffee grower/Sue Cunningham
Photographic), 40 (packaging/Adrian Sherratt), 43 (computer classroom/Les
Gibbon), 43 (remote controls/Brian Elliott), 45 (terracotta army/LMR Group),
45 (terracotta soldier/Visual Arts Library (London)), 45 (Xi'an terracotta warriors/
Marco Secchi), 46 (repaired terracotta soldiers/SAS), 46 (terracotta warriors
museum/Geoff A Howard), 49 (The Louvre/Art Kowalsky), 49 (Egyptian Museum,
Cairo/BL Images Ltd), 51 (Sabratha, Libya/imagebroker), 52 (Millau hanging
bridge, France/1Apix), 52 (Itaipu hydroelectric dam, Paraguay/Mike Goldwater),
53 (Petronas Twin Towers, Kuala Lumpar, Malaysia/one-image photography),
58 (Sydney Opera House/Rob Walls), 59 (Skylab/Mike Spence/NASA), 60
(Barcelona 1992 Olympic poster/Ace Stock Limited), 67 (FIFA World Cup/
Kolvenbach), 78 (antique telephone/Index Stock), 82 (presentation with
sign language/Jeff Greenberg); Art Directors and Trip Photo Library p22
(Islamabad Pakistan Government Buildings/Juliet Highet); Axiom Photographic
Agency p32 (forest/Jax Murray); Corbis pp4 (open book/Medioimages), 8 (school
cafeteria/TWPhoto), 9 (Japanese school exam/TWPhoto), 19 (ophthalmologist/
James Marshall), 23 (garbage truck/Michael S. Yamashita), 24 (2006 International
Consumer Electronics Show/Steve Marcus/Reuters), 26 (Mexico City/Danny
Lehman), 27 (ruins of Harappa, Pakistan/Roger Wood), 37 (freight terminal/
Jon Hicks), 54 (Palm Island, Dubai/Jorge Ferrari/epa), 62 (Travis Mayer skier/
Chris Trotman/Duomo), 82 (texting/Charles Gullung/zefa); Getty Images pp5
(students/Phil Boorman/Taxi), 29 (raindrops/amana images), 57 (Shanghai/
Mahaux Photography/The Image Bank), 79 (speaker/Bruce Ayres/Stone); OUP
pp19 (carrots/Ingram), 19 (peas/Photodisc); Panos Pictures p21 (tubular bus
station/Paul Smith); PunchStock pp13 (patient/image100), 17 (backache/
BananaStock), 33 (solar panels/Digital Vision), 51 (Machu Picchu/Digital
Archive Japan); Reuters Pictures p54 (The World, man-made islands, Dubai/
Ho New); Rex Features pp13 (harpist on ward), 61 (Olympic village/London
2012), 77 (IBM computer 1982/SB/TS/Keystone USA); Robert Harding Picture
Library p7 (Russian classroom/Sylvain Grandadam); Science and Society
Picture Library p78 (Vodafone transportable mobile phone, 1985/Science
Museum); Still Pictures pp7 (Ethiopian school/Sean Sprague), 7 (Mexican school/
Mark Edwards), 50 (Peloponnes, Nemea excavation/Mike Schroeder/argus).

Illustrations by: Mark Duffin pp 30, 69, 72